From Manager to Mentor

Conversations You Cannot Rehearse

Robert Rosenfeld

From Manager to Mentor: Conversations You Cannot Rehearse

Published by Robert Rosenfeld via Kindle Direct Publishing

First published 2026

ISBN: 978-1-0676888-0-6

Table of Contents

Preface

A brief apology ...and a longer argument

Why me?

I have spent most of my career in two worlds. As a business school academic, I researched and taught management, business strategy, international business, and entrepreneurship. As a management consultant, I work with organizations trying to make those ideas stick in practice. The gap between what the research says works and what happens in a busy manager's diary is where this book lives.

Over the years, I have been a mentor, a mentee, and occasionally both at once. I have made most of the mistakes this book warns against, including several I invented myself. I have also seen, firsthand and through research, what happens when mentoring is done well: careers accelerate, confidence builds, and organizations get measurably better at developing their people.

This book is the result of a deliberate choice. After years of advising organizations on their mentoring programs and teaching the principles in the classroom, I wanted to put the whole picture in one place: research, practice, and the honest bits that neither academic papers nor corporate training slides tend to include. If it reads like a conversation with someone who has been in the room and is willing to say what they saw, that is the intention.

Why now?

The short answer: because the job of leading people is changing faster than most leaders are keeping up with.

For decades, management operated on a broadly stable set of assumptions. Authority came with the title. Knowledge flowed downwards. Loyalty was rewarded with tenure, and career paths were linear enough that a senior manager could advise a junior one by describing their own route and saying, '*Do roughly this.*' None of that holds any longer.

The managers reading this book are leading teams that may be distributed across time zones, working hybrid patterns that did not exist five years ago, and navigating an employment market in which the most talented people have options and know it. They are managing alongside artificial intelligence tools that can draft a strategy document in minutes, but cannot tell whether the person across the table is about to resign. They are expected to deliver results, develop their people, champion wellbeing, promote inclusion, and demonstrate vulnerability, often in the same meeting. The old command-and-control playbook not only feels outdated; it actively fails.

What is replacing it is a leadership style built on influence rather than authority. On conversation, not instruction. On developing others, not directing them. That shift is not a management fad; it is a structural response to the way work, technology, and talent have changed. And it makes mentoring, the discipline of helping another person think, grow, and find their own answers, one of the most important leadership skills a manager can develop. Those conversations, unscripted, unpredictable, and impossible to rehearse in advance, are what this book is about.

This is the real reason this book exists now. Not because the world needed another book about mentoring, but because mentoring has moved from a nice-to-have activity for managers with spare time to a core leadership capability for anyone who wants to retain, develop, and get the best from the people around them. The organizations that understand this are already building mentoring into their leadership development programs. Those who do not are watching their best people leave.

If you are holding this book, you are probably already inclined to mentor. The question is not whether to do it, but how to do it well enough to make a difference: for your mentee, for your organization, and for you. That is what the next eighteen chapters are for.

Acknowledgments

Writing a book about mentoring is a bit like navigating a maze blindfolded! It's challenging, but with the right guidance, you can find your way to the center! The primary reason I have this opportunity is the countless individuals I have encountered in my career who have influenced my thoughts and actions in one form or another. Anyone who has spent time in organizations knows that learning never quite stops. This can be either reassuring or mildly exhausting, depending on the day!

Embarking on this literary journey has been an enjoyable and motivating experience: I highly recommend it, unless you have a phobia of writer's block and looming deadlines! In particular, I want to thank Andrea, my wife, for her unwavering love, patience, and encouragement to complete the book, even when I was burning the midnight oil and mumbling about mentoring strategies in my sleep. To my children, Adam & Julie, for their support while I soldiered on with this project, despite their concerns that I might start wearing tweed jackets with elbow patches and quoting Shakespeare at the dinner table. This is the third book of mine in which they appear in the Acknowledgment. I am sure they are also curious (and slightly apprehensive) about whether there will be a fourth! Joining the informal book launch is my new extended family of Luke, Hannah, Lily, Simon, Emily, Dan, William, and Sophia. My appreciation to all of you for accepting me into the family and putting up with my peculiar habit of turning every conversation into a mentoring moment!

By a conservative estimate, I owe a significant portion of my professional insights to the many thousands of students, co-faculty, clients, and colleagues that I have had the pleasure of working with over the years. I appreciate your commitment to your own learning; it definitely encouraged me to stay at the top of my game as a mentor and avoid falling into the trap of recycling old anecdotes.

Finally, I am indebted to the reviewers who generously shared their time and expertise to provide feedback on early drafts, and only occasionally suggested that I should consider a career in interpretive dance instead. To Patrick Duparcq, Steve Harris, Morven McLean, Jeremy Munday, Robin Stuart-Kotze, and Andrea Szalay, your detailed comments and suggestions have greatly improved the clarity and impact of this work. Any remaining errors, omissions, or moments of "*did he really just write that?*" are entirely my own.

1. Introduction

So, you've decided to become a mentor... What could possibly go right?

TL;DR

This book is built on a simple premise: the best mentors are skilled improvisers. They prepare thoroughly, then set the script aside and respond to what is happening in front of them. This Introduction explains why that idea matters, what mentoring can do for you (not just your mentee), and how the book is organized so you can use it your way. If you read nothing else, read the section on the skilled improviser: it is the thread that runs through every chapter that follows.

What this book is about

Mentoring is a partnership in which a more experienced person provides guidance, feedback, and support to help someone else develop their skills, confidence, and professional judgment. It is a form of accelerated learning that relies on conversation, reflection, and shared experience rather than instruction or supervision.

This is a practical book for people who mentor others at work, or who are about to. It is written for middle and senior managers who want to do the job well, not just willingly. It draws on research, but it is not an academic textbook; it draws on experience, but it is not a memoir. It is, I hope, the book I wished someone had handed me before my first mentoring conversation, which went about as smoothly as you might expect when one party has no idea what they are doing, and the other is too polite to say so.

Having served as both a mentor and a mentee throughout my career, I have learned that mentoring is less instruction and more improvisation. That observation is not a throwaway line. It is the central argument of this book.

Mentoring happens in conversation. Not in reports, not in performance reviews, not in the carefully worded email you draft and redraft before sending. The developmental work, the shift in thinking, the moment of honest self-appraisal, the decision that changes the direction of a career, happens in the room, between two people, in real time. That is what makes mentoring both powerful and genuinely difficult. You cannot prepare a script for a conversation you have not yet had. You cannot know in advance whether your mentee will arrive fired up or deflated, whether they will want a challenge or reassurance, or whether the goal they set three months ago still means what it did then. The mentoring conversation is, by its nature, unpredictable, and the mentor who tries to control it too tightly will miss what matters most.

This book takes that unpredictability seriously. Rather than offering a formula to follow, it gives you the knowledge, tools, and judgment to respond to whatever the conversation brings. The difference between a mentor who handles that well and one who doesn't is not experience or seniority. It is adaptability.

The skilled improviser

Donald Schön, in his influential study of how professionals work, found that the best practitioners rely less on formulas learned in training and more on improvisation developed through practice.[1] He called this 'reflection-in-action': the capacity to think about what you are doing while you are doing it, and to adjust your approach based on what the situation is telling you. A good doctor does not simply apply a textbook protocol to every patient. A good architect does not repeat the same design for every site. And a good mentor does not run the same conversation with every mentee.

The parallel with theatrical improvisation is worth taking seriously. Johnstone, whose work on improvisational theatre has influenced fields well beyond the stage, identified principles that translate directly into mentoring: listen to what is being said rather than waiting for your turn to speak; accept what your partner offers rather than blocking it; respond to what is happening in the room rather than what you planned for.[2]

---

[1] Schön, Donald A. 1983. The Reflective Practitioner: How Professionals Think in Action. New York: Basic Books.

[2] Johnstone, Keith. 1979. *Impro: Improvisation and the Theatre*. London: Faber and Faber

Johnstone observed that the improviser's first skill lies in releasing their partner's imagination, not in being clever themselves. Substitute 'mentee' for 'partner' and you have a working definition of what good mentoring looks like.

What makes an improviser *skilled* rather than merely unprepared is preparation. Jazz musicians practice scales for years before performing. They do not intend to play those scales on stage; they practice them so thoroughly that they can forget them when it matters and respond to the music that is unfolding. The frameworks, models, and techniques in this book serve the same purpose. You learn them not to apply them mechanically, but so that you have a repertoire to draw from when the conversation takes an unexpected turn, as it will.

This idea, that effective mentoring is adaptive, responsive, and built on judgment rather than formula, runs through every chapter. Chapter 2 develops it fully. The rest of the book is, in a sense, the practice material: the scales, chord progressions, and techniques that make improvisation good rather than chaotic. If you want to go further and practice the improvisation itself, Appendix C provides a short toolkit of exercises adapted from applied improvisation. It is the equivalent of sitting in on a jam session rather than just reading about one.

The title of this book makes a direct promise: these are conversations you cannot rehearse. That is not a counsel of despair. It is an accurate description of what mentoring requires, and a release from the pressure to get it right in advance. The skilled improviser does not walk into a session hoping to deliver a performance. They walk in prepared, curious, and ready to follow where the conversation leads.

Consider what that looks like in practice. A mentee arrives for what was scheduled as a career-planning conversation and opens with something unexpected: a difficult exchange with their manager that morning, a job offer they received yesterday, and a creeping sense that the direction they chose twelve months ago no longer feels right. The mentor who is wedded to the agenda will struggle. The one who can set it aside, follow the thread, and trust their preparation to provide the tools when needed — that mentor is useful.

None of this means winging it. The improviser's apparent spontaneity rests on serious preparation. This book is, among other things, that preparation: the frameworks, research, and techniques that give you enough of a repertoire to respond well when the conversation goes somewhere you didn't expect. Which, in mentoring, is most of the time.

Why mentor? What's in it for you?

It is natural to think of mentoring as something you do for someone else. That is half the story. The research is detailed: mentors benefit at least as much as their mentees, and sometimes more.

The evidence points to five consistent benefits for mentors. **Career development accelerates.** Mentoring signals to senior leaders that you develop others, a trait increasingly valued as you progress, and studies show that mentors experience faster promotion rates and greater career satisfaction.[3] **Leadership skills sharpen.** Through practice in a low-stakes setting, the mentoring relationship serves as a live laboratory for communication, emotional intelligence, and constructive challenge, without the high stakes of formal authority. **Job satisfaction**

---

[3] Allen, Tammy D., Lillian T. Eby, Mark L. Poteet, Elizabeth Lentz, and Lizzette Lima. 2004. "Career Benefits Associated with Mentoring for Protégés: A Meta-Analysis." *Journal of Applied Psychology* 89, no. 1: 127–136. https://doi.org/10.1037/0021-9010.89.1.127.

and sense of purpose increase. Helping someone grow provides tangible evidence of contribution that quarterly targets rarely match. **Professional networks expand.** Your mentee connects you to parts of the organization you might never otherwise engage with (think of them as your personal organizational anthropologist, reporting back from the field on what is happening several levels below you). And, finally, **cognitive growth continues**. Explaining your knowledge to someone else forces you to re-examine it: there is nothing like a mentee asking, *'But why do we do it that way?'* to reveal that you have been following a process simply because it has always been done that way.

It is rather like compound interest, but for your career, and with better odds than your pension fund. The irony is satisfying: by helping someone else develop, you often advance faster than if you had focused solely on your own progression.

What your mentee gains

Meta-analyses consistently show that mentored individuals advance more rapidly, report greater career satisfaction, and demonstrate higher performance ratings than their non-mentored peers.[4] But the most important benefits are harder to measure. A good mentor provides career clarity, helping the mentee see the arc of their professional life rather than just the next step. They build confidence that is earned through honest feedback rather than empty encouragement. They decode the unwritten rules of the organization, providing access to

---

[4] Allen, Tammy D., Lillian T. Eby, and Elizabeth Lentz. 2006. "Mentorship Behaviors and Mentorship Quality Associated with Formal Mentoring Programs: Closing the Gap between Research and Practice." *Journal of Applied Psychology* 91, no. 3: 567–578. https://doi.org/10.1037/0021-9010.91.3.567.

informal networks and organizational knowledge that no induction program covers. And they offer psychological support during the inevitable setbacks, serving as a buffer against isolation and imposter syndrome without crossing the line into therapy.

The single most valuable thing many mentees report is simply this: having someone who listens without judgment, takes their development seriously, and tells them the truth. That sounds modest. In most organizations, it is remarkably rare.

What the organization gains

Organizations with mentoring programs report higher retention, stronger internal communication, and stronger leadership pipelines.[5] Mentoring supports knowledge transfer between generations of employees, strengthens a culture of continuous development, and contributes to diversity and inclusion by giving employees from underrepresented backgrounds access to the informal networks and sponsorship that have historically been distributed unevenly. These are real benefits, but they only materialize when mentoring is done well. A poorly run program is worse than no program at all, because it consumes time and goodwill while delivering nothing. This book is designed to help you be the mentor who makes the investment worthwhile.

---

[5] Ragins, Belle Rose, and Kathy E. Kram, eds. 2007. *The Handbook of Mentoring at Work: Theory, Research, and Practice*. Thousand Oaks, CA: Sage Publications.

How this book works

The book is organized into three parts. Part 1 (Chapters 1–4) covers the foundations: what mentoring is, how it differs from coaching and managing, the different forms it takes, and what to expect from the role. Part 2 (Chapters 5–11) develops the core skills: assessing your competencies, selecting a mentee, building trust and confidentiality, working across diversity, and learning the techniques that make mentoring conversations productive. Part 3 (Chapters 12–18) addresses the practical realities: getting started, building an action plan, maintaining momentum, giving feedback, managing the transition when the relationship ends, and adapting your approach for hybrid and virtual settings.

You do not need to read the chapters in order. The book is designed for pick-and-mix reading: each chapter works as a standalone resource, so you can go directly to whatever is most relevant to your situation right now. Every chapter opens with a TL;DR ('too long; didn't read') summary to help you decide whether to read it now or return to it later and closes with a Debrief that pulls out the key points and suggests a concrete next step.

Research confirms that mentoring has a significant positive effect on mentees' adaptive performance. It can nurture their ability to respond effectively to changing demands and unfamiliar situations.[6] That, in the end, is what the skilled improviser is trying to develop: not dependence on the mentor, but the

---

[6] Zeng, Hao, Li Zhao, and Siming Ruan. 2020. "How Does Mentoring Affect Protégés' Adaptive Performance in the Workplace: Roles of Thriving at Work and Promotion Focus." *Frontiers in Psychology* 11: 546152. https://doi.org/10.3389/fpsyg.2020.546152.

mentee's own capacity to adapt. This book aims to help you do exactly that.

Debrief

The research base on mentoring is large and, on the central question, unambiguous: mentoring works. It works for mentees, mentors, and the organizations that support it. What the research is less clear about is why some mentoring relationships succeed while others drift into irrelevance, and this book tries to answer that question.

The inclusion of the skilled improviser perspective is not a gimmick. It captures something real about what separates effective mentors from well-meaning but formulaic ones. Preparation matters. Technique matters. But in the moment of the conversation itself, what matters most is your ability to read what your mentee needs and respond to it, not to what you planned to discuss, not to what worked with your last mentee, and not to what chapter four told you to do.

The five mentor benefits, career development, leadership skills, job satisfaction, expanded networks, and continued learning, are not fringe findings. They appear consistently across decades of research. If you are approaching mentoring as a selfless act of professional charity, you are underestimating what you stand to gain.

Your next step: Before you read further, ask yourself one question: honestly, without the answer you think you should give. Why do you want to mentor? If the answer is purely altruistic, that is admirable but incomplete. The best mentoring relationships work because both parties have something to gain. Knowing what you want from the experience is not selfish; it is the first step toward being good at it.

2. Mentoring, coaching & managing people

More than just free advice (but still mostly advice)

TL;DR

Mentoring is not coaching with a more senior person in the room, nor is it management with the performance targets removed. These are three genuinely different activities, each with distinct purposes and dynamics, and confusing them is one of the most common reasons mentoring relationships underperform. This chapter makes the distinctions clear: it introduces the mentor mindset, the orientations that separate genuinely effective mentors from well-intentioned ones, and explains when mentoring works and when it does not.

What is mentoring?

The word 'mentor' is approximately three thousand years old. In Homer's The Odyssey, Mentor is the trusted friend to whom Odysseus entrusts his son Telemachus before departing on his ten-year journey. What is instructive about the original story is that Mentor was not merely a teacher or guardian in the formal sense. He was a confidant, an advisor, a figure who combined knowledge with genuine care for the person in his charge. Athena, goddess of wisdom, occasionally inhabits Mentor's form to offer guidance at critical moments, a deeply meaningful metaphor for the role of multiple mentors.

The contemporary definition has lost some of that richness. The Cambridge English Dictionary describes mentoring as 'the act or process of helping and giving advice to a younger or less experienced person, especially in a job or at school.' That is accurate but thin, like describing a great meal as 'the intake of food with a view to reducing hunger.' It captures the mechanism without capturing what makes it worthwhile.

A more complete definition would acknowledge that mentoring is a developmental relationship in which a more experienced person offers guidance, perspective, and support to help someone else grow in capability, confidence, and judgment. Crucially, the relationship is confidential, voluntary, and characterized by genuine investment from both parties.

Kram's research identified two broad categories of what mentors provide: career functions, sponsorship, exposure, coaching particular skills, protection, challenging assignments, and psychosocial functions, role modeling, acceptance, counseling, and friendship.[7] They are all matter. Mentors who deliver only career guidance tend to produce technically capable mentees who remain anxious and uncertain about their worth. Mentors who offer only emotional support tend to produce confident mentees who still cannot get the promotion.

Three things that look alike, but aren't

Mentoring, coaching, and managing

Walk into most organizations, and you will find these three terms used somewhat interchangeably, sometimes by people who should know better. A manager might say they 'coached' someone when they talked them through a problem. A mentor might describe what they are doing as 'managing' their mentee's development. A coach might claim to offer mentoring. The overlap in language reflects genuine overlap in practice; all three involve conversations about performance and development, but treating them as synonyms causes real problems, because each operates on different assumptions about what the other person needs.

Mentoring

Mentoring is fundamentally about the long view. Its central question is: *who do you want to become, and what would it take to get there?* The mentor draws on their own experience and knowledge to offer a perspective that the mentee cannot yet have. The relationship is typically informal, sustained over months or years, and focused on the mentee's development as a whole person rather than on achieving specific organizational

---

[7] Kram, K.E. 1985. Mentoring at Work: Developmental Relationships in Organizational Life. University Press of America.

targets. Ragins and Cotton describe it as 'a developmental relationship that provides career and psychosocial support': the key word being that it serves the mentee's interests, not primarily the organization's.[8] This distinction becomes important when a mentee's aspirations diverge from the organization's immediate needs.

Coaching

Coaching is more focused. Its central question is: *what is stopping you from performing at your best, and what would release that potential?* A coach works with what the coachee already has: latent capability, blocked by obstacles the coach helps to identify and remove. Whitmore's formulation captures this well: coaching is about 'unlocking a person's potential to maximize their own performance.'[9] Importantly, a coach does not need to be an expert in the coachee's field. A skilled executive coach might support a neurosurgeon in their leadership without knowing the first thing about neurosurgery. The coach's value comes from the quality of the questions they ask, not the expertise they bring.

Managing people

Managing operates differently still. Its central question is: are these performance targets being met, and if not, what needs to change? Management drives results through direction, assessment, and accountability. Even the most gifted, empathetic manager operates within a hierarchical, evaluative relationship:

---

[8] Ragins, B.R. & Cotton, J.L. 1999. "Mentor functions and outcomes: A comparison of men and women in formal and informal mentoring relationships." *Journal of Applied Psychology* 84, no. 4: 529–550.

[9] Whitmore, J. 2017. Coaching for Performance: The Principles and Practice of Coaching and Leadership (5th ed.). Nicholas Brealey Publishing.

they will, at some point, be involved in decisions about their reports' pay, progression, or continued employment. This does not preclude warmth or genuine developmental intent, but it does mean that every conversation takes place against a backdrop of performance expectations.

A mentee can tell their mentor something that would never be safe to share with their line manager. This difference in psychological safety is not incidental; it is the reason mentoring exists as a separate practice at all.

A comparison at a glance

Dimension	Mentoring	Coaching	Managing
Primary focus	Long-term development of the whole person	Releasing existing potential to improve performance	Achieving assigned goals and results
Relationship dynamic	Experienced guide and developing professional, often outside the line	Facilitator and person being developed: expertise in the method, not necessarily the field	Hierarchical, the manager evaluates and directs the report
Where expertise sits	With the mentor, drawn upon as relevant	Primarily with the coachee, unlocked through questioning	With the manager, applied to performance expectations
Typical timescale	Months to years; relationship-driven	Fixed engagement around specific goals; more bounded	Ongoing; tied to role and performance cycle

Dimension	Mentoring	Coaching	Managing
What success looks like	Mentee develops clearer direction, stronger judgment, greater confidence	Specific improvement in targeted behavior or capability	Objectives met; performance standards reached
Primary risk	Mentor projects own path onto mentee; mentee becomes dependent	Overuse of questions when direct experience would serve better	Performance imperative crowds out development investment

Three scenarios

Consider the same presenting situation through the lens of each role.

A mid-level manager, Elena, tells you she is considering leaving the organization for a competitor. She respects the company but feels her development has stalled and is not certain her current trajectory will get her where she wants to be in five years.

As her line manager, your immediate priority is retention. Elena is a high performer, and losing her would create real problems. You might offer a development plan, a stretch assignment, or a conversation about her future within the team. These are well-intentioned responses, but they are constrained by the fact that your interests and Elena's are not fully aligned. She knows this. Whatever you say, she will be weighing whether you are looking after her development or treating it as a staffing problem.

As her coach, you might help Elena examine her assumptions about the competitive role, explore what she genuinely values in her work, and determine whether her restlessness stems from this organization or something deeper. A skilled coach might ask: 'What would staying look like if things were genuinely good? What would need to be different?' The coaching relationship has no stake in whether Elena stays or goes, only in whether her decision is well-considered.

As her mentor, you bring something neither of the above can easily offer: your own experience of moments when the organization felt limiting, and what you did about it. You might share, honestly, not diplomatically, what you know about the competitor, what moving at this stage of a career typically does to people, and whether the grass is as green as it currently appears. You might also ask some of the same questions a coach would ask, but you can do something a coach typically cannot: offer a perspective grounded in having been there yourself.

None of these three people is doing anything wrong. But they are doing different things, and the person who tries to do all three at once, managing, coaching, and mentoring in the same conversation, usually does none of them well.

The mentor mindset

Technique matters in mentoring, but mindset matters more. A mentor who has read every framework and can cite every model but approaches conversations with the wrong orientation will consistently produce worse outcomes than a mentor with fewer tools and better instincts.

What distinguishes genuinely effective mentors from well-intentioned but mediocre ones? Research and practice point to five orientations that separate the two groups.

Curiosity about the person, not just the problem

When a mentee arrives with a presenting concern, a difficult colleague, a missed promotion, a decision about whether to take a new role, there is always a temptation to engage primarily with the surface problem and offer solutions. The most effective mentors are more interested in the person holding the problem than in the problem itself. They ask: what is this situation revealing about where my mentee is right now, what they believe about themselves and their options, and what they might not be seeing? This orientation produces conversations that feel qualitatively different to the mentee: less like advice sessions, more like someone genuinely paying attention to them.

A bias toward questions over answers

This is not the fashionable coaching injunction to never give advice: advice has its place, and one genuine advantage of a mentor is that they have earned the right to offer it through their own experience. The point is about the default posture. A mentor who has an immediate answer to every problem the mentee raises will, over time, produce a mentee who becomes dependent on that external judgment rather than developing their own. The mentor who asks first and allows the mentee to think through the situation before offering a perspective develops something more valuable: the mentee's capacity to resolve future problems independently.

Comfort with not knowing

Effective mentors are willing to sit with uncertainty, both their own and their mentee's. There is pressure, felt by mentors and expected by some mentees, to be the person with the answers. But mentees frequently bring situations that are genuinely ambiguous, with no obviously right course of action, and where what they need is not an answer but a thoughtful companion to work through complexity. The mentor who projects false confidence in uncertain situations does not build trust; they eventually undermine it when the mentee discovers that the confident advice was wrong.

Investment in the mentee's growth rather than the mentor's influence

There is a form of mentoring that is more about the mentor's ego than the mentee's development: the need to be seen as wise, the pleasure of being turned to for guidance, the satisfaction of being an important figure in someone else's career. None of these motivations is disqualifying, but they become problems when they override the mentee's actual needs.

Ragins makes this point directly in her work on high-quality mentoring: what distinguishes the best relationships is that mentors are genuinely oriented toward the mentee's self-defined growth rather than a version of development that reflects the mentor's own values and career choices.[10]

Adaptability

This theme recurs throughout the book, but it begins here. Effective mentors do not use a fixed approach consistently across all mentees and situations. They read what is needed, adjust their tone and technique, and remain aware that what worked brilliantly with one person may be entirely wrong for another. This is the orientation of the skilled improviser, not the absence of preparation, but the willingness to set it aside when the situation calls for something different.

---

[10] Ragins, B.R. 2016. "From the ordinary to the extraordinary: High-quality mentoring relationships at work." *Organizational Dynamics* 45, no. 3: 228–244.

When mentoring works, and when it doesn't

Research on the effectiveness of mentoring is broadly positive: mentored individuals show better career outcomes, higher job satisfaction, and stronger organizational commitment than their unmentored counterparts, even after controlling for prior performance.[11] But this aggregate picture obscures considerable variation. Some mentoring relationships produce genuinely significant outcomes; others produce very little; and a meaningful minority are actively counterproductive. Understanding what creates these different outcomes is more practically useful than knowing the average.

Mentoring works best when the mentee has a clear sense of what they want to develop and the self-awareness to engage honestly with feedback. It works when the relationship has sufficient trust to allow both parties to say difficult things: when the mentor can offer an honest view the mentee may not want to hear, and when the mentee can acknowledge when the mentor's perspective is missing the mark. It works when the match creates enough common ground for rapport but enough difference to generate genuine learning. It works when both parties show up prepared, follow through between sessions, and treat the relationship as an investment rather than an obligation.

Mentoring is less effective when the mentee is unclear about what they want, shows limited readiness for feedback, or approaches sessions passively, waiting to be told what to think

---

[11] Eby, L.T., Allen, T.D., Evans, S.C., Ng, T. & DuBois, D.L. 2008. "Does mentoring matter? A multidisciplinary meta-analysis comparing mentored and non-mentored individuals." *Journal of Vocational Behavior* 72, no. 2: 254–267.

rather than actively using the conversation to develop their own judgment. It is also less effective when the match lacks sufficient rapport for honest exchange, or when organizational factors compromise the confidentiality that the relationship requires.

A more uncomfortable truth is that mentoring can be **actively harmful** in certain conditions. Scandura's research on dysfunctional mentoring relationships is sobering: mentees who experience poor mentoring, mentors who are self-serving, take credit for the mentee's work, provide inappropriate personal attention, or actively withhold opportunities, show worse career outcomes and greater cynicism than those who were never mentored at all.[12] The message is not that mentoring is risky. It is that sloppy or self-interested mentoring is worse than no mentoring, and the quality of the relationship matters far more than its mere existence.

Knowing these failure modes does not warrant excessive caution. It is a cause for honest, occasional reflection on whether a particular relationship is genuinely serving its intended purpose.

What mentoring is trying to achieve

Mentoring relationships serve different purposes at different times, and a mentor who assumes they know what their mentee needs without asking is likely to spend considerable energy solving the wrong problem. Six broad objectives are outlined below, each with a note on what it looks like in practice.

---

[12] Scandura, T.A. 1998. "Dysfunctional mentoring relationships and outcomes." *Journal of Management* 24, no. 3: 449–467.

Career guidance

Career guidance addresses the big questions: which direction to take, when to take risks, and how to build toward a longer-term vision. Whether a mentee needs help mapping the territory early in their career or weighing a specific move later, this is where the mentor's own experience carries the most weight, not as a prescription for what the mentee should do, but as a hard-won perspective on how similar situations typically unfold.

Social and emotional support

Senior roles can be genuinely isolating. There are few safe spaces in organizational life where a leader can admit to feeling out of their depth, worried about a decision, or shaken by a setback without that admission being used against them. A good mentoring relationship provides that space. The mentor who can say 'I've been there, and here is what I found useful' does something formal support structures cannot: they normalize the experience through their own history.

Skill development

Here, the conversation moves from reflection to practice. The mentor identifies gaps in the mentee's current capability, helps them understand what excellent performance in those areas looks like, and supports them in finding opportunities to practice. This is where the mentor draws most explicitly on their technical knowledge, and where the distinctions between mentoring and coaching become most blurred, both involve working on specific competencies. The difference is that the mentor brings content expertise, whereas the coach's value lies primarily in how they ask questions.

Networking

Effective mentors recognize that part of their contribution is access to people, conversations, and contexts that the mentee would struggle to reach independently. An invitation to sit in on a board presentation, an introduction to someone whose network extends in a direction the mentee needs to reach, a recommendation that opens a door otherwise closed, these are substantive contributions that a mentor with significant organizational standing is uniquely placed to make.

Knowledge sharing

Every organization has a gap between the official account of how things work and the actual practice. Technical expertise, institutional memory, understanding of how decisions really get made, familiarity with the unwritten rules that govern advancement: this kind of knowledge is rarely documented anywhere, and sharing it thoughtfully is one of the highest-value things a mentor can do.

Performance improvement

This objective brings the mentoring conversation closest to the territory of management. Here, the focus is on specific behaviors that are limiting the mentee's effectiveness: a tendency to over-control rather than delegate, difficulty managing upwards, and a communication style that creates friction with peers. Unlike feedback from a manager in a performance review, feedback delivered in a mentoring context arrives without the power differential and institutional stakes, making it easier to hear, reflect on, and more likely to result in genuine change.

The critical point is not to pick one of these objectives and stick with it. Mentee needs can shift over time and between conversations. An effective mentor pays attention to what is needed, asks when uncertain, and resists the temptation to default to whichever objective they find most comfortable.

The skilled improviser: First appearance

A metaphor that will reappear throughout this book is worth introducing here.

Jazz musicians practice scales and chord progressions for years before they ever perform, not because they intend to play those scales on stage, but because having them deeply embedded allows them to improvise freely in response to what is happening in the room. The structure lives in the background; the responsiveness is what the audience experiences.

Effective mentoring works the same way. The frameworks, models, and techniques in this book are your equivalent of scales: worth knowing thoroughly, worth practicing deliberately. But the mentoring conversation itself is improvisational. The mentee does not arrive having read your preparation notes. They bring whatever is happening for them that day, which may bear no resemblance to what you both agreed to discuss last time. And your most significant contribution will often come not from deploying the right framework at the right moment, but from having enough experience and attentiveness to recognize what the moment calls for.

This is not an argument against preparation. It is an argument about what preparation is for. You prepare so that you have options; you improvise so that you choose the right one.

Exercise: What your mentee needs

Before your next mentoring session, spend ten minutes with these questions. Where you are uncertain, note it explicitly as something to explore in the session.

1. Which of the six objectives has dominated your recent conversations?

2. Which objective has barely been mentioned, and do you know why?

3. What is your honest assessment of your mentee's current state: are they in problem-solving mode, emotional processing mode, or longer-term strategic reflection mode?

4. What have they said they want from today's conversation? What do you think they need?

5. Where is the gap between those two answers, and how will you navigate it?

The last question is the hardest and the most important. A mentee who says they want practical advice on a specific situation may need to talk through a crisis of confidence first; offering practical advice before that underlying issue is aired produces solutions they will not act on. Developing the judgment to distinguish surface requests from underlying needs is one of the core competencies of effective mentoring. It cannot be acquired from a page; it comes from paying close attention, over time.

Debrief

Three things are worth carrying from this chapter.

First, the distinctions between mentoring, coaching, and managing matter in practice, not just in theory. The manager who tries to mentor a direct report runs into structural problems that good intentions cannot resolve: the evaluative relationship is always in the room, even when neither party mentions it. The mentor who slips into directive management undermines the relationship's defining quality: its safety. Knowing which role you are in at any given moment and being honest about it is a more important competency than most mentors realize.

Second, the mentor mindset, curiosity, patience with uncertainty, genuine orientation toward the mentee's own goals rather than the mentor's image of where they should be headed, is harder to develop than any technique in this book. Most people who have been successful in organizations have developed strong preferences for action, clear direction, and visible results. Mentoring rewards different instincts: staying with a question longer than feels comfortable, resisting the urge to close ambiguity with a confident answer, and remaining genuinely curious about another person's experience without projecting your own. These instincts can be developed, but they require deliberate practice, and that practice begins with noticing when you are working against them.

Third, mentoring does not work by default. The research showing positive outcomes for mentored individuals rests on relationships in which both parties were genuinely engaged, the match created sufficient trust for honest exchange, and someone was paying attention to whether the relationship was working. None of those conditions appears automatically. They are created through deliberate attention, and that begins with knowing what you are trying to achieve.

Your next step: Review your current mentoring relationships against the six objectives. Write down what you believe each mentee most needs right now and note how you know. Then, at the start of your next session with each of them, ask whether your reading is correct. The degree of alignment between your assessment and theirs is itself diagnostic, and the gap, if there is one, often lies at the heart of the most important conversation.

3. Different forms of mentoring

So many flavors of mentorship, and none come with a manual!

TL;DR

Mentoring is not a single activity. It comes in at least seven distinct forms, each suited to different situations, and the skilled improviser knows when to reach for which. This chapter maps the territory: from the in-house mentoring most organizations default to, through career mentoring, role model relationships, and the reverse mentoring that Jack Welch made famous at GE, to peer-to-peer, group, and external mentoring. Some of these will be familiar; others may prompt you to rethink what a mentoring relationship can look like. The exercise at the end invites you to take stock of which forms you use and which you overlook.

In-house mentoring

In-house mentoring is the form most people picture when they hear the word. A more experienced person within the same organization guides a less experienced colleague: sharing knowledge, offering perspective, and helping them make sense of the unwritten rules that no induction program covers.

The advantages are obvious: both parties understand the organizational context, access is straightforward, and the mentee gains someone who can interpret the politics, culture, and career pathways that are invisible from outside. When it works well, it also benefits the organization: improving retention, strengthening communication across levels, and building a culture where development is something people do for each other rather than something that arrives in a training catalog.[13] Meta-analytic evidence confirms that employees with mentors report higher job satisfaction, stronger organizational commitment, and more promotions than those without.[14]

The risk, rarely discussed, is insularity. A mentee whose only developmental input comes from inside the same organization may absorb its assumptions uncritically. The best in-house mentors are alert to this and actively encourage their mentees to seek perspectives from beyond the organization's walls.

---

[13] Naim, Mohammad Faraz, and Usha Lenka. 2018. "Development and Retention of Generation Y Employees: A Conceptual Framework." *Employee Relations* 40, no. 2: 433–55

[14] Allen, T. D., Eby, L. T., Poteet, M. L., Lentz, E., and Lima, L. 2004. "Career Benefits Associated with Mentoring for Protégés: A Meta-Analysis", *Journal of Applied Psychology* 89, no. 1: 127–136.

Career mentoring

Career mentoring focuses specifically on professional trajectory: the big directional questions about where someone is heading, what opportunities to pursue, and what to do when the path ahead is unclear. It can happen inside or outside an organization, and it tends to operate over a longer time horizon than other forms. Kram's research distinguished two core functions of mentoring: career support (sponsorship, exposure, coaching) and psychosocial support (acceptance, counselling, friendship).[15] Career mentoring sits squarely in the first category, though in practice the two are rarely separable.

A career mentor brings something different from a line manager or a coach: the ability to step back from the immediate role and consider the whole arc. That might mean helping a mentee recognize that a lateral move is worth more than a promotion, or that the industry they trained for is no longer the one they should stay in. Ibarra's work on career transitions suggests that people do not discover new career directions through analysis alone; they discover them by experimenting with 'possible selves': trying on new roles, testing new networks, and making sense of what emerges.[16] A good career mentor creates the conditions for that experimentation.

Role model mentoring

Role model mentoring is the least formal of the forms covered here, and possibly the most underestimated. It happens when

---

[15] Kram, K. E. (1985). Mentoring at Work: Developmental Relationships in Organizational Life. Scott Foresman.

[16] Ibarra, H. (2023). Working Identity: Unconventional Strategies for Reinventing Your Career (Updated Edition). Harvard Business Press.

someone learns by observing another person, not through structured sessions, but through watching how they handle situations, make decisions, and conduct themselves professionally.

The relationship may be direct (a junior colleague consciously studying how a senior leader chairs meetings or handles conflict) or entirely at a distance (a first-generation entrepreneur modeling themselves on a founder whose interviews they have watched repeatedly). In its simplest form, the 'mentor' may not even know they are playing the role. Ibarra's research on professional identity found that people construct their professional selves by observing multiple role models and assembling a 'collage' of attributes drawn from different sources: borrowing one person's approach to client relationships, another's way of handling pressure, a third's presentation style.[17]

What makes role model mentoring worth taking seriously is that it happens whether you intend it or not. If you are a senior manager, people are already drawing conclusions from your behavior: how you respond under pressure, whether you listen before speaking, and how you treat the most junior person in the room. The question is not whether you are a role model; it is whether you are a good one. That distinction is worth sitting with.

Reverse mentoring

Reverse mentoring inverts the traditional arrangement: a more junior person mentors a more senior person. The idea gained prominence in the late 1990s when Jack Welch, then CEO of General Electric, recognized that his senior executives were

---

[17] Ibarra, H. 1999. "Provisional Selves: Experimenting with Image and Identity in Professional Adaptation." *Administrative Science Quarterly* 44, no. 4: 764–791.

falling behind on technology. His solution was to pair them with younger employees who understood the internet and its business applications. GE credited the program with accelerating innovation across the company.[18]

The concept has since spread well beyond technology skills. Luxury brands including Gucci and Louis Vuitton have used reverse mentoring to help senior leaders understand the preferences and expectations of younger consumers. Other organizations use it to give senior executives direct exposure to the experiences of employees from underrepresented groups, a more honest form of insight than anything a diversity report can provide. Recent research confirms the broader benefits: reverse mentoring has been shown to increase work engagement and improve work outcomes for both parties.[19]

Reverse mentoring works when both parties take it seriously. The junior mentor needs to feel genuinely safe to speak candidly, and the senior mentee needs to be willing to sit in the unfamiliar position of not being the expert. When those conditions are met, it can shift how an organization thinks about hierarchy, learning, and who has something worth teaching. When those conditions are absent, it becomes a performance, a box-ticking exercise that wastes everyone's time.

---

[18] Murphy, W. M. 2012. "Reverse Mentoring at Work: Fostering Cross-Generational Learning and Developing Millennial Leaders." *Human Resource Management* 51, no. 4: 549–573.

[19] Garg, N., Murphy, W. & Singh, P. 2021. "Reverse Mentoring, Job Crafting and Work-Outcomes: The Mediating Role of Work Engagement.", *Career Development International* 26, no. 2: 290–308.

Peer-to-peer mentoring

Peer-to-peer mentoring pairs people at a similar level, not for one to guide the other, but to learn from the exchange. It works because the power dynamic that shapes most mentoring relationships is largely absent. Two middle managers comparing notes on how they handle difficult team members are likely to be more candid with each other than either would be with someone two levels above them. Kram & Isabella's research on peer relationships identified three distinct types: information peers, collegial peers, and special peers, each offering different developmental functions.[20]

This form has become particularly common among entrepreneurs and startup founders, where the challenges are intense, the learning curve is steep, and the number of people who genuinely understand what you are dealing with is small. Peer mentoring groups, sometimes called mastermind groups or founder circles, provide a space where people can share mistakes without it appearing on a performance review.

The limitation is the same as the strength: without a difference in experience or perspective, peer mentoring can become a mutual support group rather than a developmental relationship. The most effective peer pairings involve people who are at a similar level but face different challenges or bring different strengths: enough common ground to build trust, enough difference to generate genuine learning.

---

[20] Kram, K. E. & Isabella, L. A. 1985. "Mentoring Alternatives: The Role of Peer Relationships in Career Development," *Academy of Management Journal* 28, no. 1: 110–132.

Group mentoring

Group mentoring brings several mentees together under the guidance of one or more mentors. It is more cost-effective than one-to-one arrangements, it exposes mentees to a wider range of perspectives, and it can create a sense of shared endeavor that individual mentoring sometimes lacks.[21]

The trade-off is depth. A mentor working with a group cannot give everyone the same attention they would receive in a one-to-one relationship. Group mentoring works best when the participants share a common context: a cohort of new managers, for instance, or a group of researchers at a similar career stage, and when the mentor is skilled at drawing out quieter members rather than letting the most confident voices dominate the conversation.

External mentoring

External mentoring involves a mentor from outside the mentee's organization. It is particularly useful when the mentee needs perspectives that their own workplace cannot provide: a broader view of their industry, honest feedback uncomplicated by organizational politics, or exposure to different ways of working.[22]

---

[21] Huizing, R. L. 2012. "Mentoring Together: A Literature Review of Group Mentoring." *Mentoring & Tutoring: Partnership in Learning* 20, no. 1: 27–55.

[22] Ensher, E. A., Thomas, C. & Murphy, S. E. 2001. "Comparison of Traditional, Step-Ahead, and Peer Mentoring on Protégés' Support, Satisfaction, and Perceptions of Career Success." *Journal of Business and Psychology* 15, no. 3: 419–438.

Many professional bodies and industry associations run external mentoring programs. Entrepreneurial mentoring schemes, where experienced business professionals advise founders and startup teams, are among the most established examples. The relationship typically involves more deliberate structure than in-house mentoring, clear objectives, agreed timescales, and explicit conversations about what each party expects, precisely because the two people do not share an organizational context that would otherwise provide a natural framework.

Virtual mentoring

Virtual mentoring is not a separate form of mentoring in the way that peer-to-peer or group mentoring is a distinct relationship. It is better understood as a 'delivery' context within which any of the other forms can operate. An in-house mentoring pair who rarely share an office, a reverse mentoring relationship conducted across time zones, a career mentor working with a mentee in a different city: all of these are, in practice, virtual mentoring relationships.

The shift to hybrid and remote working has made this the default for a significant proportion of mentoring pairs, rather than an occasional workaround. That shift brings specific challenges. Building rapport without physical presence, reading the room through a camera, maintaining momentum without the natural rhythm of in-person meetings: these are worth treating seriously rather than assuming good face-to-face mentoring simply transfers across unchanged.

Because those challenges are substantial enough to warrant their own treatment, Chapter 17 addresses virtual and hybrid mentoring in full. It covers what changes, what stays the same, how to structure sessions for the medium, and how to manage the technology without letting it get in the way of the conversation.

Exercise: Your mentoring range finder

Most mentors default to one or two forms of mentoring and use them with everyone. This exercise is designed to make that pattern visible.

Below are the seven forms of mentoring covered in this chapter. For each one, ask yourself two questions: first, have I used this form in the past twelve months? Second, could any of my current mentees benefit from it?

Form of mentoring	Used in the past 12 months?	Could a mentee benefit?	If yes: Which mentee, and why?
In-house mentoring			
Career mentoring			
Role model mentoring			
Reverse mentoring			
Peer-to-peer mentoring			
Group mentoring			
External mentoring			

If your answers cluster around in-house and career mentoring, and most people's do, that is not a failing. It simply means you have a wider range of approaches available than you are currently using. Pick one form you have not tried and consider how you might introduce it with a mentee who could benefit.

Debrief

Higgins and Kram's influential reconceptualization of mentoring argued that individuals benefit most not from a single mentor but from a 'developmental network': multiple relationships, serving different functions, drawn from different parts of their professional life.[23] Their research found that the variety of mentoring sources mattered as much as the quality of any individual relationship.

The seven forms described in this chapter are not competing alternatives. They are different tools, suited to different situations, and the mentor who knows only one of them is working with an unnecessarily limited range. Reverse mentoring, where the junior party teaches the senior one, deserves particular attention, not necessarily because it is fashionable, but because it is one of the few arrangements that genuinely challenge a senior leader's assumptions rather than reinforcing them.

The exercise makes a simple but often-overlooked point clear: most mentors default to one or two forms and apply them regardless of the mentee's needs. If every relationship you have looks the same, the issue is probably not your mentees: it is your range.

The skilled improviser's question is not 'which form of mentoring do I prefer?' but 'which form does this person, in this situation, need from me right now?' That question is worth revisiting with every mentee you work with.

---

[23] Higgins, M. C. & Kram, K. E. 2001. "Reconceptualizing Mentoring at Work: A Developmental Network Perspective." *Academy of Management Review* 26, no. 2: 264–288.

Your next step: Look at the exercise you have just completed. Choose one form of mentoring you have not used recently and identify one mentee who might benefit from it. Then try it, not as a grand experiment, but as a single conversation where you approach the relationship a little differently.

4. Expectations of being a mentor

Keeping the spark alive (without setting fire to your mentee)

TL;DR

Before you volunteer for another mentoring relationship, let's be honest about what you're signing up for. This is not a quick favor; it is a sustained commitment requiring regular, focused conversations over months or years. But mentoring is not professional charity: research consistently shows that mentors gain greater job satisfaction, stronger organizational commitment, and higher perceived career success than colleagues who do not mentor. This chapter explores realistic expectations and introduces the Career Vision Statement.

What you are signing up for

Think of mentoring as tending a garden rather than painting a fence: it requires regular attention over an extended period, not intensive effort in a single afternoon. Most effective mentoring relationships involve monthly or bimonthly conversations, providing enough frequency to build momentum while respecting the reality that both parties have demanding day jobs. Some pairs find their rhythm with less frequent but longer sessions; others prefer shorter, more regular check-ins. The right cadence is whatever both parties can sustain consistently.

The critical threshold appears to be around twice-yearly: drop below it, and you are essentially starting from scratch each time, unable to build on previous conversations or track meaningful progress. If you cannot commit to at least quarterly meetings, you should not commit to the relationship. That is not a criticism; it is an honest assessment of what mentoring requires. A mentee who is repeatedly rescheduled learns only one thing: that their development is a lower priority than whatever displaced it.

Ivey and Dupré, in their critical review of workplace mentoring, note that the benefits of mentoring are real but conditional; they materialize in circumstances for particular people and require a genuine investment of time and attention. Mentoring is not a transaction; it is a relationship, and relationships that receive sporadic attention tend to produce sporadic results.[24]

---

[24] Ivey, Gary W., and Kathryne E. Dupré. "Workplace Mentorship: A Critical Review." *Journal of Career Development* 49, no. 3 (2022): 714–29. https://doi.org/10.1177/0894845320957737.

What you stand to gain

Mentoring is sometimes framed as an act of generosity, the experienced professional giving back to the next generation. That framing is not wrong, but it is incomplete. A substantial body of research now shows that the benefits to mentors are as real as those to mentees, and in some cases, more pronounced. Meta-analytic evidence confirms that mentors report significantly higher job satisfaction and organizational commitment than non-mentoring colleagues, as well as greater perceived career success and stronger job performance.[25] Ivey and Dupré confirmed these findings in their comprehensive review, noting that positive outcomes for mentors include reduced turnover intention and increased engagement[26].

Five benefits stand out in the research and in the experience of practicing mentors:

Personal and professional growth is the most reported benefit. Mentoring compels you to articulate knowledge that might otherwise remain tacit: the assumptions, judgments, and pattern-recognition that experienced professionals use instinctively but rarely examine. In the process of explaining your thinking to someone else, you sharpen your own understanding of it. Several mentors have told me that preparing for mentoring sessions forced them to stay current in their fields in ways their day jobs no longer demanded.

---

[25] Ghosh, Rajashi, and Thomas G. Reio Jr. "Career Benefits Associated with Mentoring for Mentors: A Meta-Analysis." *Journal of Vocational Behavior* 83, no. 1 (2013): 106–16. https://doi.org/10.1016/j.jvb.2013.03.011.

[26] Ivey and Dupré, "Workplace Mentorship: A Critical Review," 714–29.

Improved leadership skills follow naturally. Mentoring develops the same capacities that define effective leadership: listening carefully, asking the right questions, providing honest feedback, and motivating someone without resorting to positional authority. Unlike managing a direct report, where the organizational hierarchy does some of the motivational work for you, mentoring requires you to be genuinely useful; there is no other reason for the mentee to keep showing up.

Increased job satisfaction is one of the more robust findings in the mentoring literature. Mentors consistently report that seeing their mentees develop gives them a sense of purpose and professional meaning that their day-to-day responsibilities may not always provide. For mid-career and senior professionals whose advancement has slowed, mentoring can reignite a sense of contribution that pure operational work sometimes fails to deliver.

Expanded networking is often overlooked. Your mentee inhabits a different part of the organization, a different generation, or a different professional network. Through them, you gain access to perspectives, information, and connections that would not otherwise reach you. This is not a calculated benefit; it is simply what happens when two people at different career stages take each other seriously.

Leaving a legacy is the benefit that mentors tend to mention last but value most. When your career reaches a stage where you have accumulated more than you can use, the question shifts from "*What can I achieve?*" to "*What can I pass on?*" Mentoring is one of the few professional activities that genuinely allows you to shape the next generation of leaders, and the impact often outlasts everything else on your CV.

What does mentoring cost you?

Honesty about costs matters because mentors who underestimate the commitment fade out after three months. The direct time investment is typically one to two hours per month, including the session itself and preparation time. That is modest by any standard, but it is time that competes with every other demand on your diary, and it requires a particular kind of attention that is different from chairing a meeting or reviewing a report.

The less visible cost is emotional. Mentoring well means being genuinely present, listening to problems you cannot solve, watching someone make mistakes you could prevent, and resisting the urge to take over. It means sitting with ambiguity; sometimes you will leave a session without knowing whether anything useful happened. For action-oriented managers accustomed to solving problems and moving on, this can be genuinely uncomfortable.

The return on that investment is not always immediate. Some mentees will take your most carefully crafted insight and completely ignore it, then six months later, attribute the same idea to someone else. Others will develop in ways you did not anticipate and will not credit you for. If you need visible, attributable results to sustain your motivation, mentoring will test you. If you can tolerate the delay and the ambiguity, the rewards for both you and your mentee are considerable.

Staying engaged when it gets difficult

Even the most committed mentors face moments when enthusiasm wanes. Competing priorities accumulate, sessions feel repetitive, and the mentee's progress, if there is any, seems invisible. The strategies that sustain engagement are not complicated, but they do require intention.

Set realistic goals from the outset. A mentoring relationship with no defined purpose will drift, and a drifting relationship is one you will quietly deprioritize. Establish clear, realistic objectives early. What does the mentee want to achieve, and what do you hope to learn? Revisit them regularly. When both parties know what they are working toward, sessions have direction; when they don't, sessions become pleasant but increasingly optional conversations.

Build a genuine personal connection. Mentoring relationships that operate purely at a professional level, exchanging advice without establishing trust, tend to produce shallow engagement from both parties. Invest time in understanding who your mentee is, not just what they do. Know their ambitions, their anxieties, their life outside work. Connection sustains effort in a way that professional courtesy alone cannot.

Celebrate incremental progress. Most development is gradual and therefore easy to miss. Make a deliberate practice of noticing and naming change: "*Six months ago, you wouldn't have handled that conversation the way you just described. What shifted?*" This serves both the mentee's confidence and your own sense of purpose.

Keep developing yourself. The moment you stop learning as a mentor, the relationship becomes one-directional, and one-directional relationships lose energy. Seek feedback from your mentee, connect with other mentors, read widely, and reflect on what is and isn't working. Garringer and Benning found that mentor satisfaction was highest among those who viewed the relationship as mutually developmental rather than as a one-way transfer of wisdom.[27]

Practice honest self-care. Setting boundaries around your time, acknowledging when you are overcommitted, and recognizing the signs of mentoring fatigue are not weaknesses; they are the conditions for sustained effectiveness. A mentor who is perpetually stretched thin is not modeling good practice; they are modeling the overcommitment that their mentee should learn to avoid.

Good mentoring practice

The strategies above keep you engaged. This section addresses what you are trying to achieve while you are engaged. Good mentoring is not about transferring your experience to someone else's career. It is about developing your mentee's capacity to think for themselves: to become self-aware, self-directing, purposeful, and resilient.

A mentee who has been well mentored can honestly evaluate their own strengths and weaknesses, rather than relying on others to tell them. They can make career decisions based on their own judgment rather than defaulting to whatever their mentor (or manager, or peers) suggests. They have a clear sense of what they want and why they want it. They have experienced enough success and enough failure to know that both are survivable and instructive.

---

[27] Garringer, Michael, and Chelsea Benning. Who Mentored You? *A Study Examining the Role Mentors Have Played in the Lives of Americans over the Last Half Century*. Boston: MENTOR: The National Mentoring Partnership, 2023.

If your mentee is becoming more dependent on you over time rather than less, something has gone wrong. The goal of mentoring is to make yourself unnecessary: not immediately, not dramatically, but progressively. A mentee who cannot make a career decision without checking with you first has not been mentored; they have been managed by someone without positional authority.

Starting with clarity

One practical tool to help a mentoring relationship get off to a purposeful start is to ask the mentee to complete a Career Vision template before your first meeting. The template invites them to articulate their aspirations, strengths, development needs, and the support they are seeking. It serves as the basis for your first conversation and gives you concrete material to work with rather than an awkward "*So... what would you like to talk about?*" opening.

Depending on the context, a mentee may be more or less able to complete the template in advance. Some will send a polished document; others will bring rough notes to the meeting for discussion. Both approaches work: the point is that the mentee has done some thinking before you meet, not that the thinking is perfect. Bear in mind that this is an initial effort, and that views and even career direction can change. Treat it as a starting point, not a contract.

Another way to use the Career Vision template is to complete one for yourself. You might complete it with the benefit of hindsight, reflecting on where you were at a similar career stage, so that your mentee gains insight into your own development journey. Alternatively, once mutual trust is established, you might complete the template as of today and discuss your current career vision with your mentee. This kind of reciprocal disclosure signals that development does not stop at a certain level of seniority and models the vulnerability you are asking of them.

Exercise: Career Vision

<table>
<tr>
<td rowspan="2">A career vision statement describes what the world might look like and feel like as a result of your professional work. A clear, compelling vision can have a magnetic effect – prioritizing choices and pulling you towards it as you focus on your work.

Your vision statement will answer: "WHAT do I want to be part of in 5 years' time?"

My Vision Statement:

Why do you want to achieve this?</td>
<td rowspan="2">Strengths & Weaknesses.
Strengths are those factors that accelerate your trajectory towards your vision. Weaknesses are those factors that may hold you back from attaining your vision. When thinking about your weaknesses, it's important to view yourself from other people's perspectives because other people tend to notice things about you that you are blind to. Although this can be an uncomfortable task, it's vital that you see yourself as realistically as possible. To this end, it's important to ask people who know you best what areas you need to improve.</td>
<th>Strengths</th>
<th>Weaknesses</th>
</tr>
<tr>
<td>• What are you better at than other people?
• What do other people view as your strengths?
• How much experience do you have in your profession?
• What skills, abilities, knowledge, or connections do you have that others don't?
• What values do you live by that most people find too demanding?
• Which professional achievements are you proudest of?</td>
<td>• What do other people say your weaknesses are?
• Which activities do you avoid doing, and why do you dislike doing them?
• Do you struggle with anxiety, imposter syndrome, or procrastination?
• Are there gaps in your education, skills, or training?
• Are you afraid to take risks?</td>
</tr>
</table>

Exercise: Pre-commitment check

Before agreeing to mentor someone new, take five minutes to answer these questions honestly. They are designed to surface the practical realities that good intentions tend to obscure.

---

1. Do I have a realistic hour per month, plus preparation time, that I can protect consistently for at least the next six months?

2. Am I genuinely interested in this person's development, or am I agreeing because it was difficult to say no?

3. Do I have relevant experience or perspective to offer for what this mentee needs? (Not all good mentors are the right mentor for every mentee.)

4. Am I willing to be challenged, disagreed with, and occasionally told that my advice was not helpful?

5. What do I hope to gain from this relationship? (If the honest answer is "nothing, " reconsider; one-way relationships rarely sustain themselves.)

If you answered yes to all five, you are ready. If one or two gave you pause, address them before you commit, ideally by discussing them with the prospective mentee. If three or more were difficult, this may not be the right time to take on a new mentoring relationship, and saying so honestly is a greater kindness than agreeing and then fading out.

Debrief

Research consistently shows that mentors who report high satisfaction share one trait: they established clear, realistic goals for the relationship from the outset. Without that clarity, mentoring becomes another obligation competing for already scarce time rather than an energizing investment in someone's future. Ivey and Dupré's comprehensive review confirmed that mentoring's benefits, greater job satisfaction, stronger organizational commitment, and higher perceived career success, are real, but they are conditional on the quality of the relationship, not merely on its existence.[28]

This chapter outlined five tangible benefits you'll gain as a mentor, but it was equally honest about the costs: the time, the emotional investment, the tolerance for ambiguity, and the willingness to watch someone develop at their own pace rather than yours. The strategies for staying engaged, setting goals, building connection, celebrating progress, continuing your own development, and practicing self-care aren't optional extras. They are the difference between mentoring relationships that thrive and those that quietly fade after the third rescheduled coffee.

The Career Vision template offers a practical starting point. By asking your mentee to articulate their aspirations before your first meeting, you ensure they have given serious thought to what they want and give yourself material to work with from day one.

Your next step: If you're considering taking on a new mentee, complete the pre-commitment check first. If you're already

---

[28] Ivey, Gary W., and Kathryne E. Dupré. "Workplace Mentorship: A Critical Review." *Journal of Career Development* 49, no. 3 (2022): 714–29. https://doi.org/10.1177/0894845320957737.

mentoring someone, ask yourself when you last revisited the goals you set together. If the answer is "*never*" or "*I can't remember,*" that conversation is overdue. And if you haven't yet completed a Career Vision template yourself and shared it with your mentee, try it; vulnerability builds trust faster than advice ever will.

5. Enhancing mentoring competencies

Turns out "Winging it" isn't actually a competency

TL;DR

The mentoring literature has been busy. Across decades of research, thousands of relationships studied, and enough academic papers to keep a small team of PhD students occupied indefinitely, a clear pattern has emerged: effective mentors don't rely on instinct alone. They develop a specific set of competencies that can be learned, practiced, and, crucially, refined. This chapter introduces a research-grounded framework that draws on the most rigorously validated instrument in the field, the Mentoring Competency Assessment (MCA), and adapts it for the realities of business leadership. Part 1 walks you through six core competencies, sequenced by how consistently they appear across the literature. Part 2 helps you identify which of them deserve your attention right now and gives you a practical toolkit to act on them.

Here's a thought experiment. Imagine asking a surgeon how they know they are performing well. They would probably cite measurable outcomes, such as complication rates, recovery times, and patient feedback. Now ask a manager how they know they're mentoring well. Most would offer something vague about 'good conversations' and 'a feeling that things are going in the right direction.'

This isn't criticism; it reflects that most managers enter mentoring without an explicit framework for what good looks like. That gap matters. Research consistently shows that mentor effectiveness is not primarily a function of experience, seniority, or good intentions. It is a function of specific, learnable competencies: behaviors that can be developed, measured, and improved.

The good news is that you do not need a doctorate in organizational psychology to benefit from this knowledge. You just need a practical map. This chapter provides one.

Part 1: The core competency framework

What the research tells us

The six competencies below are drawn primarily from the Mentoring Competency Assessment (MCA): a validated, 26-item instrument tested across 283 mentor–mentee pairs at 16 universities and recognized as one of the most psychometrically robust tools in the mentoring literature.[29] The MCA identifies six core

---

[29]Fleming, M., House, S., Shewakramani, V., Yu, L., Garbutt, J., McGee, R., and Rubio, D.M. "The Mentoring Competency

mentor competency domains: maintaining effective communication, aligning expectations, assessing understanding, addressing diversity, building independence, and promoting professional development.

A word of transparency is warranted here. The MCA was developed and validated in academic research mentoring: specifically, mentoring early-career clinical and translational researchers. If you are a business leader rather than a laboratory director, you might reasonably ask what that has to do with you.

The interpersonal dynamics of mentoring (communication quality, the risk of dependency, the role of trust, the challenge of giving useful feedback) are not fundamentally different in a business context. The competencies the MCA identifies have since been corroborated across healthcare, professional services, and corporate leadership development. That said, academic research mentoring does not map neatly onto business leadership: a research mentor's primary concern is scientific independence, while a business mentor's concerns are more varied and commercially grounded. The framework below retains the MCA's validated structure while adapting its framing and examples for corporate and professional life. Where the adaptation involves genuine interpretation rather than straight translation, the relevant footnote says so.

The sequence below reflects how frequently each competency appears across the broader workplace mentoring literature, from Kram's work on mentoring functions[30] through Allen et

---

Assessment: Validation of a New Instrument to Evaluate Skills of Research Mentors." *Academic Medicine* 88, no. 7 (2013): 1002--8.

[30] Kram, K.E. 1985. Mentoring at Work: Developmental Relationships in Organizational Life. Scott Foresman.

al.'s meta-analysis of 43 studies[31] to more recent systematic reviews. Those near the top appear in virtually every serious treatment of mentor effectiveness; those towards the bottom are well evidenced but more context-dependent.

One caveat worth stating plainly: these competencies interact. A highly self-aware mentor who is poor at communication clearly understands the relationship's dynamics but fails to act on that understanding. A mentor skilled in communication but low in adaptive intelligence communicates fluently with people like them and struggles with everyone else. The framework is a diagnostic tool, not a hierarchy.

Competency 1: Communication mastery

The foundation of everything else

If the mentoring literature agrees on nothing else, it agrees on this: effective mentors are exceptional communicators. Communication mastery appears in virtually every competency framework, instrument, and research review in the field, making it the most consistently cited mentor competency across the literature.

But 'good communication' has been so thoroughly overworked by leadership development programs that it has lost most of its meaning. In a mentoring context, it is more specific and more demanding than its reputation suggests. It begins with active listening: not the polite nodding-while-waiting-to-speak variety, but genuine, disciplined attention to what the mentee is

---

31 Allen, T.D., Eby, L.T., Poteet, M.L., Lentz, E., & Lima, L. 2004. "Career benefits associated with mentoring for protégés: A meta-analysis." Journal of Applied Psychology 89, no. 1: 127–136.

saying, how they say it, and what they choose not to say. Research on listening behavior suggests that most people retain only about a quarter of what they hear. Effective mentors work hard to close that gap.

It extends into questioning: the ability to ask questions that open thinking rather than close it, that explore rather than lead, and that invite the mentee to do the intellectual work rather than outsourcing it to the mentor. Moving from broad, exploratory questions to more focused ones, as earlier chapters describe, the 'questioning funnel' is one practical application of this principle.

And it includes the often-underrated skill of paraphrasing: reflecting back what you have heard in your own words, both to confirm understanding and to help the mentee hear their own thinking from a slight distance. Experienced mentors know that paraphrasing is not just a listening technique: it is frequently the moment when a mentee has their most significant insight of the conversation.

Competency 2: Self-awareness and empathy

Knowing yourself well enough to get out of the way

The second most consistently cited competency cluster combines two qualities that are intimately connected: self-awareness and empathy.[32] They are treated together here because one without the other produces a particular and recognizable variety of mentoring problems. Self-awareness without empathy

---

[32] Cherniss, C. 2007. The role of emotional intelligence in mentoring. In Ragins & Kram (Eds.), op. cit.; see also Goleman, D. 1998. *Working with Emotional Intelligence*. Bloomsbury.

produces a mentor who has done extensive personal reflection and then applies it as a template for everyone they mentor (*'I know my own blind spots, let me watch out for yours too.*') Empathy without self-awareness produces the opposite: a mentor who is genuinely attuned to their mentee's emotional experience but unconsciously allows unexamined biases to shape their guidance.

Together, however, these qualities form the relational intelligence that underpins the relationship. Self-aware mentors notice when their own history colors their advice: when what they suggest is what they would do, not necessarily what the mentee should do. Empathetic mentors can track the emotional register of a conversation even as they manage its content and adjust.

Here is the data point that tends to stop rooms cold: research suggests that 95% of people believe they are self-aware, while assessments indicate that only 10–15% demonstrate measurable self-awareness.[33] That gap lives somewhere, and some of it is in every mentoring relationship currently running. Developing genuine self-awareness is not a one-time exercise: it is an ongoing discipline that requires external input, honest feedback, and the intellectual humility to act on what you learn.

Competency 3: Building mentee autonomy

The art of making yourself unnecessary

Here is a competency that runs directly counter to many managers' instincts. Most people chosen to mentor someone are

---

[33]Eurich, T. 2017. Insight: Why We're Not as Self-Aware as We Think, and How Seeing Ourselves Clearly Helps Us Succeed at Work and in Life. Crown Business.

selected precisely because they have relevant experience and sound judgment. The temptation, entirely understandable, is to apply that experience as directly and efficiently as possible. To give clear advice. To share what worked. To tell people what to do.

Effective mentors resist this temptation. Not because their experience is irrelevant, but because building the mentee's capacity to think independently, make their own decisions, and develop their own judgment is more valuable in the long run than any specific advice the mentor can offer. Allen's research on mentor motivation identified this as a critical differentiator between mentors who produce lasting impact and those who produce dependency.[34][35]

The mentee who leaves a mentoring relationship able to solve their own problems is far better served than one who leaves needing to consult their mentor before every significant decision.[36]

In practice, building autonomy means asking rather than telling. It means asking '*what options are you considering?*' before sharing your own view. It means tolerating a mentee's decision to take a path you would not have recommended and supporting them through it rather than waiting to say, '*I told you so.*' And it means recognizing that the goal of mentoring is not to

---

[34]Allen, T.D. 2007. Mentoring relationships from the perspective of the mentor. In Ragins & Kram (Eds.), op. cit.

[35]Allen, T.D. 2003. "Mentoring others: A dispositional and motivational approach." *Journal of Vocational Behavior* 62, no. 1: 134–154.

[36]Ragins, B.R., Cotton, J.L., & Miller, J.S. 2000. "Marginal mentoring: The effects of type of mentor, quality of relationship, and program design on work and career attitudes." *Academy of Management Journal* 43, no. 6: 1177–1194.

produce a more effective version of yourself. It is to produce a more effective version.

Competency 4: Clarity and alignment

Making sure you are both watching the same film

The fourth competency addresses one of the most common and preventable sources of failure in mentoring relationships: misaligned expectations. Research on mentoring relationship quality consistently identifies a misalignment of expectations regarding the relationship's purpose, frequency, boundaries, and outcomes as a primary driver of dissatisfaction on both sides.

This competency operates at two levels. The first is structural: ensuring that both parties share a clear understanding of what the mentoring relationship is for, what it is not for, how often they will meet, and what success looks like. This is the territory covered by the contracting chapter in this book, and it is essential.

The second level is more dynamic: the ongoing checking of understanding that occurs within individual conversations. Effective mentors regularly pause to confirm they have understood what the mentee is trying to communicate, not just what the words said, but what was meant. This is particularly important in conversations about complex career decisions or emotionally charged situations, where the distance between what someone says and what they mean can be considerable.

The MCA's framing of 'assessing understanding' is useful because it captures both directions of this competency: the mentor's understanding of the mentee, and the mentor's ability to check that the mentee has understood what the mentor has offered. Both matter, and both are routinely underinvested.

Competency 5: Championing growth

Playing the long game

The fifth competency is perhaps the most distinctively mentor-like of the six: actively promoting the mentee's long-term professional development. This extends well beyond the goals discussed in individual conversations: it encompasses a broader orientation towards the mentee's trajectory, potential, and future opportunities.

Mentors who champion growth think beyond the immediate presenting issue. They take a longer view of where their mentee is heading and actively seek ways to advance that journey: making introductions, advocating internally, highlighting development opportunities the mentee might not have noticed, and helping them see their own strengths more clearly than they can on their own.

This is the sponsorship function that Kram originally identified alongside the psychosocial support function of mentoring,[37] and it remains one of the most reliably impactful things a senior mentor can offer. Research on career outcomes consistently shows that mentees with active sponsors, mentors who do more than offer counsel, experience significantly better career progression than those in purely advisory relationships.[38]

The caveat is worth stating clearly: championing growth requires a clear-eyed view of the mentee's actual capabilities and potential, not merely an enthusiastic one. Advocating for

---

[37]Kram, K.E. 1985. op. cit.

[38]Hewlett, S.A., Marshall, M., & Sherbin, L. 2011. The Sponsor Effect: Breaking Through the Last Glass Ceiling. Harvard Business Review Research Report.

someone beyond their current abilities can damage both their reputation and yours. The skill lies in calibrating ambition to evidence.

Competency 6: Adaptive intelligence

Mentoring the person in front of you, not a generic version of them

The final competency underpins all the others. Adaptive intelligence, the ability to recognize and respond to the full range of differences between you and your mentee, is what separates mentors who are effective across a wide range of people from those who are effective primarily with people like themselves.

Those differences include the obvious demographic dimensions, gender, ethnicity, age, cultural background, but extend far beyond: different cognitive styles, communication preferences, relationships with hierarchy and authority, and career frameworks shaped by very different professional histories.

Research on mentoring across differences suggests that demographic similarity is not the primary driver of relationship quality.[39] What matters more is whether the mentor is aware of the differences, genuinely curious about their implications, and adaptive enough to adjust their approach. A mentor with high adaptive intelligence can form effective relationships across a wide range of differences; one who unconsciously filters mentees through the lens of their own experience cannot.

---

[39]Ragins, B.R. 2002. Understanding diversified mentoring relationships. In D. Clutterbuck & B.R. Ragins (Eds.), *Mentoring and Diversity*. Butterworth-Heinemann.

Earley and Ang's Cultural Intelligence (CQ) framework is useful here[40]: particularly the distinction between cognitive CQ (knowing about differences), motivational CQ (caring enough to adapt), and behavioral CQ (adapting in practice). Most experienced managers score reasonably well on the first. The second and third are where the development work tends to live.

Part 2: Your personal competency profile

Stop. Do not skip this part. Part 1 gave you the map. This part asks you to figure out where on it you are, which is, if we are being straightforward about it, considerably more useful than being able to describe the terrain in the abstract. The exercise below is deliberately different from a traditional self-assessment. There are no scales to score, no totals to add up, and no color-coded indicators telling you whether you have passed. Research on self-assessment in professional development contexts consistently shows that numerical ratings tend to produce flattering distortions: people score themselves higher than their behavior warrants, particularly for socially valued competencies. What produces more accurate and more useful self-knowledge is behavioral evidence: specific memories of actual conversations, concrete examples of what you did and did not do. The diagnostic questions below ask for exactly that. Your job is not to rate yourself. It is to recall.

---

[40]Earley, P.C. & Ang, S. 2003. Cultural Intelligence: Individual Interactions Across Cultures. Stanford University Press.

The diagnostic: Six competencies, six honest conversations with yourself

For each competency, the questions below are designed to surface specific evidence from your actual mentoring practice. Work through them with a particular mentee relationship in mind: ideally, one that is active and reasonably developed, so you have enough material to draw on. If you are new to formal mentoring, think about conversations where you were acting in a guidance or development role, even informally.

Resist the urge to answer in generalities. 'I think I'm pretty good at listening' is not evidence. 'In my last session, I asked three questions and gave four minutes of advice' is evidence.

Communication mastery

In your last three mentoring conversations, who spoke more: you or your mentee? If you are genuinely unsure, that is already a data point worth sitting with.

Can you recall a specific moment when you noticed something in how your mentee was communicating, a hesitation, a shift in tone, an unusual word choice, and followed it rather than moved on? When did you last paraphrase something back to a mentee and have them respond with 'yes, exactly', or, more usefully, 'no, that's not quite it'? What did you do with that correction?

Self-awareness and empathy

Think about a mentee whose challenges are quite different from anything you have personally experienced. How do you approach those conversations: with genuine curiosity, or with a quiet skepticism about experiences that do not map onto your own?

When did you last change your approach mid-conversation after noticing the mentee's emotional state shifting? And when did you last give advice that, on reflection, said more about what you would do than what your mentee needed?

Building mentee autonomy

What is the approximate ratio of advice to questions in your typical session? When a mentee presents a problem, what is your default instinct: to explore their thinking, or to offer your own?

Think of a recent situation where your mentee decided you would not have made. Did you support them through it, or did you find a way to revisit your original position? And here is the harder question: do any of your current mentees come to you primarily to get confirmation for decisions they have already made? If so, what does that tell you about the dynamic?

Clarity and alignment

If you asked your current mentee right now what the primary goal of your mentoring relationship is, would their answer match yours? How often do you explicitly check whether the relationship is still serving their actual development needs, or has the agenda drifted on autopilot?

In individual conversations, when a mentee says something complex or ambiguous, do you tend to ask for clarification or tend to assume you have understood? Think of the last time you assumed, and were wrong.

Championing growth

Outside your regular sessions, in what concrete ways are you actively contributing to your mentee's development? Have you made an introduction, created an opportunity, or advocated for them in the past six months?

Do you know what your mentee's next significant career aspiration is, and have you taken any action to help them move towards it? If a colleague asked you about your mentee's strengths and potential right now, how specific and compelling would your answer be?

Adaptive intelligence

How similar are you to your current mentee in background, career path, communication style, and general outlook? If the answer is 'very similar, ' is that a coincidence or a pattern?

When did you last actively ask a mentee about their perspective on something rather than assuming you understood it? Can you recall a moment when you adjusted your approach mid-relationship because you recognized that your default style wasn't working well for this person?

Building your development plan

If you have honestly worked through the diagnostic, you should have a reasonably clear sense of where your strengths lie and where the gaps are. The temptation at this point is to try to develop everything simultaneously, which is the professional development equivalent of taking up marathon running, sourdough baking, and conversational Mandarin in the same month. It tends to produce limited progress across all fronts and significant frustration.

Instead, identify your single highest-priority competency: the one where the gap between your current practice and where you want it to be is both significant and most consequential for your mentees. Then choose one or two tactics from the menu below. Commit to them specifically; a tactic without a defined first step is merely a good intention.

Tactics for communication mastery

Keep a brief post-session log noting the approximate ratio of talking to listening. If you consistently log more talking than listening, try a constraint: no advice until the mentee has fully articulated their own view of the problem.

Seek feedback from a trusted colleague on your listening habits. Specifically, self-reports of listening behavior are notoriously unreliable.

Tactics for self-awareness and empathy

Identify one aspect of your approach that you suspect might be more about your preferences than your mentee's needs: a topic you steer towards, a type of solution you reach for. Consciously withhold that preference for three sessions and notice what changes.

Consider a 360-degree feedback exercise that includes your mentoring relationships. The gap between self-assessment and external perspectives is often instructive.

Tactics for building mentee autonomy

Introduce a simple rule into your practice: before sharing any opinion or recommendation, ask two questions. Not one, always two. This forces genuine exploration before advice-giving and, once habitual, tends to produce significantly better conversations.

Review your last three sessions and count how many times you gave explicit advice versus how many times you asked the mentee what they thought. If the ratio is heavily skewed towards advice, you have identified your development frontier.

Tactics for clarity and alignment

Build a structured review of your mentoring relationship, at least quarterly, by stepping back from the content of individual sessions and explicitly discussing whether the relationship remains focused on your mentee's needs. Treat this as a scheduled agenda item, not an optional extra.

Prepare one clarifying question per session: something you would normally assume you understood but could check productively. Use 'I think I know what you meant' as an invitation to confirm, not a reason to move on.

Tactics for championing growth

Commit to one non-session-based action for each mentee per quarter: an introduction, a recommendation, a conversation with a relevant stakeholder. Track whether you follow through. The sponsorship dimension of mentoring is the most consistently impactful on career outcomes, yet the most neglected because it requires initiative outside the regular meeting pattern.

Define what 'championing' looks like for each mentee individually. For some, it means visibility, for others, access. Ask them directly.

Tactics for adaptive intelligence

Seek out reading, reflection, or conversation that gives you genuine insight into experiences different from your own, not to achieve mastery, but to develop the habit of active curiosity about perspectives that do not mirror yours. Treat misunderstandings, moments when a mentee indicates you have missed something, as learning opportunities. If your mentoring relationships tend to cluster among people like you in background or style, consider whether you are challenging yourself to operate outside your adaptive comfort zone often enough.

Debrief

Competency frameworks have a slightly unfortunate history in management development: they proliferate, overlap, and eventually collapse under their own bureaucratic weight into something resembling a job description. This chapter has sought to offer something more useful: a framework grounded in the strongest available evidence, adapted for a business context, and structured for use.

The six competencies are not a checklist to be completed and filed. They are a recurring diagnostic: something to return to periodically and ask, with genuine honesty, 'what has changed?' The mentors who develop most rapidly are not those who score highest on an initial assessment. They are the ones who keep interrogating their own practice long after the initial novelty of reflection has worn off.

If you have identified a priority development area and committed to one tactic, that is a meaningful start. If you have committed to two, that is appropriately ambitious. If you have committed to all six, please revisit the marathon-and-sourdough paragraph above.

Your next step: Before your next mentoring session, re-read your answers to the diagnostic questions for the one competency you rated most honestly: the one where the evidence was thinnest, not the one where you felt most comfortable. Then set yourself a single, observable test for that session: one specific behavior you will either do or consciously refrain from doing, depending on what the diagnostic told you. Not a new philosophy. Not a development plan. Just one thing, in one conversation, to see what changes. If the answer surprises you, that is the chapter doing its job.

6. Selecting a mentee

Why "they seemed nice" is not a matching strategy

TL;DR:

Choosing a mentee is a bit like choosing a travel companion for a long and occasionally turbulent journey. Pick someone purely because they seem familiar or convenient, and you may find yourself wondering eighteen months later why the trip felt unrewarding for both of you. This chapter dispels the notion that matching on shared background or professional similarity reliably predicts success. What matters is more interesting: shared values, compatible expectations, and whether your potential mentee has the disposition for the honest, occasionally uncomfortable work that good mentoring demands. Spoiler: not everyone does!

Most mentors give surprisingly little thought to who they mentor. A colleague asks, a program coordinator assigns someone, or a direct report expresses interest at the right moment, and the relationship begins. This is not necessarily a bad outcome. Some of the most productive mentoring relationships start opportunistically. But leaving selection entirely to circumstance means leaving one of the most significant variables in the mentoring equation entirely to chance.

The decision about who to mentor deserves more deliberate attention than it typically receives. This is not because mentors should be precious about their time, but rather a poor match wastes it. A relationship that never quite finds its footing, where the mentor's experience doesn't align with the mentee's needs, or where the two parties' commitment levels are simply misaligned, tends to drift rather than develop. Both parties end up going through the motions, each mildly guilty about the sessions they keep rescheduling.

There is also a more uncomfortable truth worth stating plainly. Mentoring requires genuine investment from the mentor: intellectual, emotional, and temporal. That investment is only sustainable when the mentor finds the relationship genuinely engaging. This is not selfishness; it is realism. A mentor who has reluctantly taken on a mentee they have little connection with, out of obligation or social pressure, will struggle to bring the quality of attention the relationship demands. The mentee deserves better, and so does the mentor. None of this means turning mentee selection into a lengthy assessment, it means approaching the question with the same thoughtfulness you would bring to any significant professional commitment.

What the research says about matching

Ask most managers how they would go about selecting a mentee, and they will describe some version of the same process: find someone who reminds them of themselves at an earlier stage, works in a similar field, or shares enough common ground to make conversation comfortable. The instinct is understandable. It is also, according to recent research, largely misguided.

The distinction that matters is between surface-level and deep-level similarity. Surface-level similarity covers the visible and easily measurable: shared professional background, industry experience, organizational seniority, and demographic characteristics. Deep-level similarity refers to something less obvious but more predictive: shared values, attitudes, and beliefs about work, development, and the purpose of a mentoring relationship. Tuma & Dolan's 2024 study of over 500 doctoral mentoring relationships found that surface-level demographic similarity was not significantly associated with relationship quality, whereas shared attitudes and values were strongly predictive of both support and satisfaction.[41] The finding challenges a widely held assumption and has direct practical implications for how mentors approach the selection process.

This does not mean that professional relevance is irrelevant. A mentor whose experience bears no relationship to the mentee's context will struggle to offer credible guidance. But relevant experience is a threshold condition, not a differentiator. Once

---

[41] Tuma, Trevor T., and Erin L. Dolan. 2024. "What Makes a Good Match? Predictors of Quality Mentorship Among Doctoral Students." CBE: Life Sciences Education 23 (2): ar20.

that threshold is met, the question shifts from "do we share a background?" to "do we share enough of a worldview to have productive, honest conversations?" Those are very different filters, and the second one is harder to assess from a CV.

The diversity research adds a further complication worth acknowledging. There is a reasonable body of evidence suggesting that cross-cultural and cross-demographic mentoring pairs can generate genuine creative and developmental benefits, precisely because the absence of shared assumptions forces both parties to examine things they might otherwise take for granted. The key condition, as Chapter 8 of this book discusses, is that the mentor approaches difference with genuine curiosity rather than either false equivalence or unwitting bias. Diversity in a mentoring pair is neither an automatic advantage nor an automatic obstacle. It is, like most things in mentoring, something that requires active and thoughtful management.

The practical implication is straightforward: when selecting a mentee, look beneath the surface. A strong match on paper, same industry, similar career stage, overlapping technical expertise, is a reasonable starting point, but it tells you relatively little about whether the relationship will work. The conversations that follow matter far more than the credentials that precede them.

The five principles of good matching

Knowing that deep-level similarity matters more than surface characteristics is useful in theory. Translating that insight into practice requires a more concrete set of criteria. The following five principles provide a working framework: not a checklist to score, but a set of considerations to keep in mind when assessing whether a potential mentoring relationship is worth pursuing.

Aligned goals and expectations. The single most reliable predictor of a productive mentoring relationship is whether both parties want the same things from it (or at least compatible ones). A mentor who sees their role as challenging assumptions and pushing the mentee beyond their comfort zone will frustrate a mentee who came looking for reassurance and a sounding board. Neither expectation is wrong; the mismatch is the problem. The solution is to surface expectations explicitly and early, before either party has invested significant time. A direct question, "*What would make this relationship genuinely useful to you in twelve months' time?*", tells you more about fit than any amount of background research.[42]

Shared values. This is subtler than aligned goals, and considerably harder to assess in a preliminary conversation. Shared values do not mean identical views, a mentoring relationship in which both parties agree on everything is unlikely to generate the productive friction that drives real development. What matters is a sufficient overlap in fundamental beliefs about how people should be treated, how organizations work, and what professional integrity looks like. A mentor who has built their career on transparency and directness will struggle to work effectively with a mentee who regards information as currency and ambiguity as a strategic tool. The gap is not unbridgeable, but it requires naming rather than ignoring.[43]

Relevant experience and expertise. This is the most obvious criterion and the one most mentors apply first, sometimes to the

---

[42] Lankau, M.J. & Scandura, T.A. 2002. "An investigation of personal learning in mentoring relationships: Content, antecedents, and consequences." *Academy of Management Journal* 45, no. 4: 779–790.

[43] Tuma, Trevor T., and Erin L. Dolan. 2024. "What Makes a Good Match? Predictors of Quality Mentorship Among Doctoral Students." *CBE - Life Sciences Education* 23 (2): ar20.

exclusion of everything else. Relevant experience matters: a mentee navigating their first board-level role benefits from a mentor who has been there, and a mentor whose entire career was in manufacturing may have limited credibility advising someone in financial services. But relevance is a starting condition rather than a sufficient one.

Productive difference. The instinct to match on similarity is natural but limiting. Research consistently shows that mentoring pairs who differ in background, perspective, or experience, and who engage with that difference constructively, tend to generate more creative thinking and more honest challenge than those who share too much common ground. The operative word is constructively. The difference that is acknowledged and explored becomes an asset; the difference that is ignored or navigated around becomes an obstacle. When assessing a potential match, the question is not whether differences exist, they always do, but whether both parties have the disposition to treat those differences as a source of insight rather than discomfort.[44]

A shared commitment to the process. Mentoring requires consistent investment from both parties: preparation before sessions, follow-through between them, and the willingness to have occasionally uncomfortable conversations. A mentee who arrives unprepared, reschedules habitually, or treats the relationship as a periodic check-in rather than a developmental commitment will exhaust even the most patient mentor. Assessing this in advance is difficult, intentions are easy to declare

---

[44] Zachary, L.J. & Fischler, L.A. 2022. *The Mentor's Guide: Facilitating Effective Learning Relationships* (3rd ed.). San Francisco: Jossey-Bass.

and hard to verify, but the preliminary conversation usually offers some signal.[45]

Having the initial conversation

The preliminary meeting between a mentor and a potential mentee is one of the most consequential yet underused tools in the entire mentoring process. Most people treat it as a formality, a getting-to-know-you coffee before the real work begins. In practice, it is an assessment, and both parties should approach it as one.

For the mentor, the conversation serves three purposes simultaneously: establishing enough rapport to enable an honest exchange, surfacing the information needed to assess fit against the five principles above, and reading the signals that indicate whether this person is disposed to make good use of mentoring. None of these can be rushed, which is why a preliminary meeting squeezed into thirty minutes between other commitments rarely tells you what you need to know.[46]

The questions worth asking are less technical than they might appear. "What are you hoping this relationship will do for you that your current role isn't doing?" is more revealing than any question about career goals. "*Tell me about a time you received feedback that genuinely changed how you approached something*" surfaces both reflective capacity and receptiveness to challenge. "*What would make you feel this relationship had been a waste of your time?*" is slightly provocative, and precisely for that reason, the

---

[45] De Janasz, S.C. & Godshalk, V.M. 2013. "The role of e-mentoring in protégés' learning and satisfaction." *Group & Organization Management* 38, no. 6: 743–774

[46] Clutterbuck, D. & Megginson, D. 2004. *Techniques for Coaching and Mentoring*. Oxford: Butterworth-Heinemann

answer is usually instructive. A mentee who responds thoughtfully is demonstrating the kind of self-awareness that mentoring depends on. One who struggles to answer at all may be seeking something the relationship cannot provide.[47]

Alongside the explicit content of the conversation, a skilled mentor pays attention to signals that indicate a learning orientation, the disposition to develop rather than simply perform. These are not criteria to score, but qualities to notice.

The first is reflective capacity: whether the mentee can step back from their own experience and examine it honestly. This usually becomes apparent within the first twenty minutes. A mentee who describes their career in terms of what happened to them, rather than the choices they made and the lessons they drew, may find the introspective demands of mentoring uncomfortable rather than energizing.

The second is receptiveness to being stretched. Some people seek mentoring for validation, they want a senior colleague to confirm that they are on the right track. Others want a genuine challenge. The two are not incompatible, but a mentee who responds to mild challenge in the preliminary conversation with defensiveness rather than curiosity is signaling something worth taking seriously.[48]

The third is comfort with ambiguity. Skilled improvisers, in mentoring as in jazz, need to operate without a script. A mentee who is only comfortable when there is a clear right answer will

---

[47] Zachary, L.J. & Fischler, L.A. 2022. *The Mentor's Guide: Facilitating Effective Learning Relationships* (3rd ed.). San Francisco: Jossey-Bass

[48] Tuma, T.T. & Dolan, E.L. 2024. "What makes a good match? Predictors of quality mentorship among doctoral students." *CBE - Life Sciences Education* 23, no. 2: ar20

find the open-ended, exploratory nature of good mentoring sessions frustrating. Watch how they talk about uncertainty: do they describe it as a problem to be resolved, or as a condition to be worked with?[49]

The fourth is evidence of learning from setbacks. Not resilience in the generic sense, but something more specific: whether this person has encountered difficulty and drawn something useful from it rather than simply enduring it. A brief question, "*What's the most useful mistake you've made in the last two years?*", usually separates those who have genuinely reflected from those who are performing reflection.[50]

The fifth is intrinsic motivation. Is the mentee pursuing the relationship because they genuinely want to develop, or because it looks good on a performance review? This is harder to assess directly, but usually apparent from the quality of their preparation. A mentee who arrives having thought carefully about what they want, and who asks as many questions about the mentor's approach as they answer about their own goals, is demonstrating the kind of engagement that makes the investment worthwhile for both parties.[51]

None of this amounts to a pass/fail assessment. The preliminary conversation is not an interview and approaching it as one will kill the rapport that makes an honest exchange possible. It is

---

[49] Dweck, C.S. 2017. Mindset: Changing the Way You Think to Fulfill Your Potential (updated ed.). London: Robinson

[50] Mezirow, J. 1991. *Transformative Dimensions of Adult Learning*. San Francisco: Jossey-Bass.

[51] Sancheznieto, Fátima, Pamela Asquith, Adriana Baez Bermejo, Emma A. Meagher, and Christine E. Pfund. 2024. "Mentoring Up for Early Career Investigators: Empowering Mentees to Proactively Engage in Their Mentoring Relationships." *Journal of Clinical and Translational Science* 8 (1): e86.

better understood as a calibration exercise: the mentor forming a considered view of whether this person, at this stage of their development, is likely to benefit from what this relationship can offer. That judgment requires both the questions and the willingness to sit with the answers, including the uncomfortable ones.

Which brings the mentor to the question they would most prefer to avoid: *what if the honest answer is no?*

Declining to take on a mentee is not a rejection of the person: it is a recognition that a poor fit matters, and that a poorly matched relationship serves neither party. A direct but respectful conversation, "*I don't think I'm the right mentor for what you're describing, but here is who I think might be*", is considerably more useful than proceeding out of obligation and delivering a mediocre experience over twelve months. The mentee who hears that honest assessment and uses it to find a better match is already learning something valuable about the importance of fit. That, in its own way, is mentoring too.

Dealing with a mismatch

Even the most carefully considered match can go wrong. Shared values and aligned goals are good predictors of relationship quality, but they are not guarantees. People change, circumstances shift, and what looked like a productive pairing at the outset can gradually or suddenly reveal itself to be something less than that. Knowing how to handle a mismatch is as important as knowing how to avoid one.

The first and most skipped step is simply acknowledging that a problem exists. Most mentors are reluctant to name difficulties in a relationship they have voluntarily taken on, it feels like an admission of failure or a criticism of the mentee they are supposed to support. The result is that mismatches often persist long past the point where either party is getting meaningful value, sustained by a combination of politeness, inertia, and the faint hope that things will improve on their own. They rarely do. Scandura's research on dysfunctional mentoring relationships found that early acknowledgment of relational difficulties was one of the clearest differentiators between relationships that recovered and those that deteriorated: the longer the problem went unnamed, the harder it became to address.[52]

Once the mismatch is acknowledged, at least privately, the next step is diagnosis. Not all mismatches are the same, and the response should fit the cause. A mismatch rooted in misaligned expectations is different from one caused by a breakdown in trust, which is different again from one driven by circumstantial change: a shift in the mentee's role, a change in the mentor's availability, or an evolution in the mentee's goals that has moved them beyond what this relationship can offer. Treating all mismatches as the same problem produces generic solutions that address none of them well.[53]

For mismatches rooted in unclear or misaligned expectations, the most common category, a direct conversation is usually sufficient. This does not need to be a formal review or a difficult confrontation. A simple observation, raised early and without blame, is enough to open the door: "I want to make sure our sessions are as useful as possible for you, I've been wondering whether what we're focusing on is still the right fit for where

---

[52] Scandura, T.A. 1998. "Dysfunctional mentoring relationships and outcomes." *Journal of Management* 24, no. 3: 449–467

[53] Eby, L.T., McManus, S.E., Simon, S.A. & Russell, J.E.A. 2000. "The protégé's perspective regarding negative mentoring experiences: The development of a taxonomy." *Journal of Vocational Behavior* 57, no. 1: 1–21.

you are now." That question invites recalibration without implying criticism and gives the mentee the opportunity to redirect the relationship before either party has invested further in the wrong direction.[54]

Where the mismatch runs deeper, where there has been a loss of trust, a boundary overstepped, or a gradual erosion of engagement that recalibration alone will not fix, the mentor may need to seek external guidance. Program coordinators, if a formal program is in place, are the obvious first port of call. An experienced colleague or a trusted peer mentor can also provide a useful outside perspective. The instinct to manage the problem privately and avoid involving others is understandable, but it is worth resisting. A fresh perspective on a relationship that has become stuck often reveals options that neither party could see from the inside.[55]

Flexibility in approach is worth attempting before concluding that a relationship has run its course. Sometimes what appears to be a fundamental mismatch is a methodological mismatch rather than a substantive one: the mentor's style is not working for this mentee, even if the underlying relationship is sound. Adjusting the format of sessions, shifting the balance between challenge and support, or changing the frequency of meetings can make a significant difference without requiring either party to start again from scratch.[56]

---

[54] Zachary, L.J. & Fischler, L.A. 2022. *The Mentor's Guide: Facilitating Effective Learning Relationships* (3rd ed.). San Francisco: Jossey-Bass.

[55] Clutterbuck, D. 2014. *Everyone Needs a Mentor* (5th ed.). London: CIPD

[56] De Haan, E. & Nilsson, V.O. 2023. "What can we know about the effectiveness of coaching? A meta-analysis based on self-reports from

If none of this works, if the relationship has genuinely run out of road, then reassignment is a legitimate and responsible outcome. This should be handled with care, in consultation with program coordinators where relevant, and framed honestly but constructively for the mentee. A relationship that ends because the fit was wrong is not a failure on either side. It is data: about what this mentor can offer, about what this mentee needs, and about how to make a better match next time. The mentor who treats it as such, rather than as an embarrassment to move past quickly, will find that even a difficult ending has something useful in it.

What can organizations do?

Most of what has been discussed in this chapter assumes individual choice. In many organizations, however, mentoring relationships are assigned: matched by HR departments or program coordinators working from spreadsheets, pairing on seniority, functional area, or availability rather than the deeper criteria that predict relationship quality.

Organizations running formal programs face real constraints: they need to match dozens or hundreds of pairs simultaneously, and they cannot require every potential pair to have a preliminary conversation before confirming. But practical constraints do not excuse poor design. The research is clear that matching quality is one of the strongest predictors of mentoring outcomes: stronger than program structure, training provision, or organizational support.[57]

---

coaches and their clients." *Consulting Psychology Journal* 75, no. 3: 185–204

[57] Garvey, B., Stokes, P. & Megginson, D. 2021. *Coaching and Mentoring: Theory and Practice* (4th ed.). London: Sage

Four steps can significantly improve organizational matching. First, gather richer data at enrollment: values, working style, attitude toward challenge, not just goals and experience.[58] Second, build a preliminary conversation into the program as a standard step rather than an optional one.[59] Third, create a low-stakes check-in at six weeks to normalize recalibration or reassignment before making any significant investment.[60] Finally, treat match data as a learning resource, systematically reviewing which pairings worked and why. Chapter 11 covers the design of formal mentoring programs in more detail.

Debrief

Selecting a mentee well is one of the most consequential decisions a mentor makes, and one of the least examined. Most mentors give it far less thought than they give to what happens once the relationship is underway, which is understandable but mistaken. A relationship built on a poor match will require considerably more effort to sustain than one where the fit was right from the start, and will rarely produce the same quality of outcome, however hard both parties work at it.

The research reviewed in this chapter challenges widely held assumptions about what constitutes good matching. Surface-level similarity, shared background, industry, seniority,

---

[58] Tuma, T.T. & Dolan, E.L. 2024. "What makes a good match? Predictors of quality mentorship among doctoral students." *CBE - Life Sciences Education* 23, no. 2: ar20

[59] Zachary, L.J. & Fischler, L.A. 2022. *The Mentor's Guide: Facilitating Effective Learning Relationships* (3rd ed.). San Francisco: Jossey-Bass

[60] Eby, L.T., Allen, T.D., Evans, S.C., Ng, T. & DuBois, D.L. 2008. "Does mentoring matter? A multidisciplinary meta-analysis comparing mentored and non-mentored individuals." *Journal of Vocational Behavior* 72, no. 2: 254–267

demographic characteristics, turns out to be a poor predictor of relationship quality. What matters more deeply: shared values, compatible expectations, and the mentee's disposition to engage in the kind of open-ended, challenging, occasionally uncomfortable work that good mentoring demands. These things cannot be assessed from a CV or an organizational chart. They emerge from conversation, which is why the preliminary meeting is not a formality but a diagnostic tool, and why the questions asked in that meeting matter as much as anything that follows.

The concept of learning orientation deserves particular emphasis. Mentoring places genuine demands on the mentee: for reflection, honesty, and the willingness to be stretched. A mentee who lacks the disposition to meet those demands will not be well served by mentoring, regardless of the mentor's skill. Identifying that disposition early is not gatekeeping. It is responsible practice.

Mismatches, when they occur, are not failures. They are information. Handled well, acknowledged early, diagnosed accurately, and addressed directly, they can be recalibrated or, where necessary, resolved without lasting damage to either party. The mentor who treats a difficult match as data rather than as embarrassment and uses it to refine their approach to selection next time is demonstrating exactly the kind of reflective practice that this book argues for throughout.

Your next step: Before agreeing to take on your next mentee, schedule a preliminary conversation of at least forty-five minutes with no agenda other than mutual assessment. Prepare three questions that you would find genuinely difficult to answer yourself: about goals, values, and attitude toward challenge, and ask them. Pay as much attention to how the mentee responds as to what they say. Then sit with the conversation for twenty-four hours before deciding. The mentor who rushes to "yes" because the mentee seems promising, or to "no" because the conversation was slightly awkward, is not yet making the decision the relationship deserves.

7. Confidentiality & privacy

What happens in mentoring stays in mentoring

TL;DR

Confidentiality is not a courtesy extended to mentees. It is the structural condition that makes mentoring worth having. Without it, conversations stay in safe territory: the kind that sounds like development but produces none. This chapter covers the psychological mechanisms underlying confidentiality and trust, the distinction between assumed and agreed confidentiality, and the practical question of scope: what stays in the room and when something might not. Trust is accumulated through consistent small behaviors over time, and damaged far more quickly than it is built. Finally, conflicts of interest deserve attention: they are more common than most mentors acknowledge, and ignoring them does not make them go away.

Why confidentiality works

The reason confidentiality matters is not primarily ethical: it is psychological. When people believe that what they say will stay in the room, they say different things. Edmondson's research on psychological safety in teams demonstrated that the conditions most predictive of candid communication and genuine learning are those in which people feel they can speak without fear of judgment, embarrassment, or reprisal.[61] The mentoring relationship offers exactly those conditions, but only when both parties deliberately create them.

In most organizational settings, people engage in continuous impression management. They share successes and struggle with setbacks. They offer opinions they think will be received well and withhold those they think will not. They present competence and conceal uncertainty. None of this is dishonest in any meaningful sense: it is simply how professional life works, and experienced managers have become very good at it.

Mentoring's potential lies in interrupting that pattern. A mentee who feels genuinely safe will tell a mentor about a leadership decision they quietly regret, a relationship with a peer that has become unworkable, or a career direction that no longer excites them. These are the real conversations, and a mentoring relationship that stays in the safe zone is significantly less valuable than one that gets underneath the surface.

The mechanism is simple to state and demanding to create. Edmondson's later work on psychological safety showed that its presence or absence is determined almost entirely by the

---

[61] Edmondson, A.C. "Psychological Safety and Learning Behavior in Work Teams." *Administrative Science Quarterly* 44, no. 2 (1999): 350--83.

behavior of the more senior or powerful person in the relationship.[62] In a mentoring relationship, that person is the mentor. If the mentor is confidential, consistent, and non-judgmental, the conditions for openness develop over time. If not, they do not, and no amount of assurance that 'this is a safe space' will compensate for a single instance of information leaking out of the room.

Assumed versus agreed confidentiality

Most mentoring relationships operate on the assumption of confidentiality. Neither party explicitly discusses what they will keep to themselves; both assume the other has the same understanding. This works well enough when both assumptions are identical, and causes significant harm when they are not.

A mentor who assumes that sharing a mentee's career concerns with HR, in the interest of being helpful, is obviously acceptable behavior will be surprised by the mentee's reaction. The mentee, who assumed that the conversation was entirely private, will experience it as a betrayal. Both people are behaving in good faith. The problem is that they never agreed.

Johnson & Ridley, in their work on the ethics of mentoring relationships, argue that confidentiality should be an explicit, early conversation rather than an assumed condition, not because mentors are untrustworthy, but because 'assumed' confidentiality is whatever each party imagines it to be, while agreed

---

[62] Edmondson, A.C. 2018. The Fearless Organization: Creating Psychological Safety in the Workplace for Learning, Innovation, and Growth. John Wiley & Sons.

confidentiality is something both parties understand in the same way.[63]

In practice, this conversation is brief and need not feel legalistic. Its purpose is simply to surface and align assumptions before a misalignment causes damage. The exercise at the end of this chapter provides a structured approach for doing this well.

What stays in the room: understanding scope

'What is said in the room stays in the room' is a useful shorthand, but it papers over a question that merits more careful thought: what exactly is being kept confidential, and from whom?

In most mentoring relationships, the answer involves at least three layers.

The content of conversations: what the mentee shares, what they are working through, what they have disclosed about their circumstances, relationships, or aspirations. This is the clearest case: the specifics of what a mentee says to a mentor should not be shared with colleagues, managers, HR, or anyone else in the organization, absent explicit consent or the exceptional circumstances discussed below.

The existence of specific topics: even without sharing details, a mentor who tells a colleague, 'We talked about some issues with the leadership team' has breached something. The mentee's choice of what to bring to mentoring is itself private.

---

[63] Johnson, W.B. & Ridley, C.R. 2018. The Elements of Mentoring (3rd ed.). St. Martin's Press.

A mentor who signals to a mentee which territory they have been exploring, even obliquely, compromises the relationship.

The mentor's own disclosures, confidentiality runs in both directions. When a mentor shares a personal setback, a mistake, or a vulnerability they have acknowledged, that information belongs in the relationship. A mentee who repeats a mentor's disclosure, even admiringly, has broken a trust that the mentor may have taken considerable personal risk to extend.

It is worth making this bidirectional quality explicit with mentees early on. The relationship is confidential in both directions: what the mentor shares is as protected as what the mentee shares, and this symmetry helps create genuine reciprocity rather than a one-sided dynamic of confession and guidance.

The limits of confidentiality

Confidentiality in mentoring is near-absolute but not unconditional. Mentors who have not thought through the exceptions before they arise will be poorly placed to handle them when they do, and the pressure of an unexpected disclosure, with no framework ready, is not the moment at which careful ethical reasoning tends to emerge.

There are four categories of situations in which confidentiality may need to yield to other obligations.

Safeguarding and serious harm

If a mentee discloses information suggesting a serious risk of harm, to themselves or to others, the mentor faces a genuine conflict between two legitimate obligations: confidentiality to the mentee and a duty of care toward those at risk. There is no universally right answer to this tension, but the professional consensus in most contexts is that immediate risk to life or safety takes precedence.[64] The keyword is serious. A mentor who escalates every disclosure of stress, unhappiness, or difficulty because it might constitute risk will quickly destroy the conditions that make mentoring work. The question to ask is not 'is this person struggling?' but 'is there a credible and immediate risk of serious harm that would not be addressed without disclosure?'

Mentors who are not trained in safeguarding should resist both extremes, dismissing concerning disclosures as 'not my problem' and over-reacting to ordinary disclosures of difficulty. If in genuine doubt, most organizations have a designated safeguarding lead or equivalent and consulting them confidentially about a hypothetical scenario (without naming the mentee) is a reasonable first step.

Legal obligations

Some disclosures create legal obligations that override confidentiality. The clearest examples are disclosures that relate to ongoing criminal activity, serious regulatory breaches, or significant financial misconduct. A mentor who learns through a mentoring conversation that their mentee is engaged in fraud or is aware of a serious safeguarding failure that has not been reported is in difficult territory.

The practical advice is straightforward: know your organization's whistleblowing and reporting policy before you need it; be honest with mentees at the outset that legal obligations limit confidentiality; and take professional advice rather than making unilateral judgments about complex situations. The

---

[64] Ragins, B.R. & Verbos, A.K. 2007. Positive relationships in action: Relational mentoring and mentoring schemas in the workplace. In Dutton, J.E. & Ragins, B.R. (Eds.), Exploring Positive Relationships at Work. Lawrence Erlbaum Associates.

mentor's role does not extend to knowingly facilitating concealment of serious wrongdoing.

Program reporting requirements

Formal organizational mentoring programs sometimes include reporting requirements: periodic updates to HR, participation logs, and outcome assessments. These do not typically require disclosure of conversation content, but they do mean the relationship is not entirely private in its existence or broader outcomes. This should be part of the initial confidentiality conversation. A mentee who discovers mid-relationship that their participation has been reported to HR, even in the most anodyne terms, will experience it as a surprise that could have been avoided.

The mentor's own need for support

This one is less often discussed but practically significant. Mentoring involves hearing difficult things, carrying complex information, and occasionally sitting with disclosures that are distressing to receive. Mentors who have no outlet for this, no supervision, no peer group, no mechanism for reflection, are at greater risk of burnout and poorer mentoring. They are also at risk of inadvertently breaching confidentiality because unprocessed material often surfaces in unexpected places.

Many professional coaching and mentoring bodies recommend, and in some contexts require, supervision for practicing mentors: regular conversations with an experienced third party focused on the mentor's own practice. Where this is available, it provides a legitimate and protected outlet. Where it is not, mentors should, at a minimum, be deliberate about how they handle the emotional content of their mentoring conversations, rather than simply absorbing it without reflection. The point is not to debrief the session content with a colleague over lunch, which directly breaks confidentiality. It is to have somewhere to put its weight.

Building trust: the dynamic view

Trust in a mentoring relationship is not something established in a single conversation. Mayer, Davis, & Schoorman's model of organizational trust identifies three components: the trustee's *ability* (do they have the competence to help?), their *benevolence* (do they genuinely have my interests at heart?), and their *integrity* (are they consistent, honest, and guided by principles I respect?).[65] All three take time to establish, and each can be undermined by a single significant failure.

The asymmetry is worth sitting with. Trust is built incrementally through dozens of small interactions, following through on a commitment, remembering something mentioned in passing three months ago, offering honest feedback without softening it into uselessness, admitting uncertainty rather than performing confidence. It is damaged dramatically, in a single moment, a confidence broken, a commitment not met, a response that reveals the mentor was not listening as carefully as they seemed.

The practical implication is to treat trust-building not as a goal to be achieved and then assumed, but as an ongoing practice. The question is not '*have I built enough trust?*' but '*what did I do in this session that either added to or subtracted from the account*?'

Establishing expertise, without reciting your CV

Mentees need to know that their mentor has something genuinely relevant to offer, a reasonable prerequisite for taking

---

[65] Mayer, R.C., Davis, J.H. & Schoorman, F.D. 1995. "An integrative model of organizational trust." *Academy of Management Review* 20, no. 3: 709–734.

someone's perspective seriously. The challenge is that most experienced professionals are either too reticent or too eager, turning early sessions into lengthy accounts of their own careers.

The most effective approach is to let expertise emerge through specificity rather than assertion. A mentor who says 'I've had a lot of experience with stakeholder management' is less convincing than one who responds to a specific situation with a precise, experience-grounded observation. Show, rather than announce.

Consistency, the discipline of small commitments

The easiest trust-building behavior, and the most reliably neglected. If you say you will send an article, send it. If you say you will think about something between sessions, show up having thought about it. If you commit to a time and date, protect it.

None of this is remarkable behavior: it is simply what reliable people do. But in organizational environments where everyone is overstretched and cancellations are routine, the mentor who demonstrably does what they say they will do accumulates trust faster than any amount of empathetic listening. The mentee notices.

Reliability under pressure

Consistency in easy conditions does not reveal much. Reliability under pressure, when the mentor is busy, when a session goes to uncomfortable places, when the honest response is difficult to give, is more diagnostic. A mentor who delivers candid feedback with care when it would be easier to stay vague, who reschedules a canceled session promptly rather than letting it drift, who stays present through a difficult conversation rather than moving toward safer ground, this is the mentor a mentee will trust with the important things.

Openness and authentic self-disclosure

This is the dimension most mentors find hardest. A mentor who presents themselves as a person of uniformly good judgment and consistent achievement will receive a mentee who does the same, producing polished, sanitized conversations about polished, sanitized versions of both parties' experiences.

Authentic self-disclosure, sharing a failure, acknowledging an uncertainty, describing a situation you handled less well than you could have, changes the atmosphere more quickly than almost anything else. It signals that the relationship is a space for honest reflection rather than performance, and it models the behavior you are asking your mentee to take risks with.

The caveat is proportion. Self-disclosure should be purposeful: offered to serve the mentee's development, not for therapeutic purposes. The test is simple: whose needs does this disclosure serve?

Respecting boundaries and knowing where they are

Mentoring involves conversations that can go deep into personal identity, confidence, values, and significant relationships. A mentor who is attentive to the cues a mentee gives about where they are and are not willing to go will build a relationship characterized by genuine safety.

The failure mode runs in both directions. A mentor who avoids anything personal keeps the relationship superficial. A mentor who pushes into territory the mentee has not opened up, probing questions about family circumstances or psychological history, has crossed a line that many mentees will not explicitly name but will act on by becoming more cautious in subsequent sessions. Watch the cues; if someone deflects, follow their lead.

Openness to feedback about your mentoring

This final dimension is the one most consistently avoided. Asking a mentee how the relationship is working, genuinely asking, then listening to the answer without becoming defensive, is both a trust-building behavior and a diagnostic tool. Mentees who feel the relationship is not meeting their needs will rarely say so unprompted; they will simply become less engaged, less open, and eventually less present. [66] Periodic, direct invitation, '*What would make our conversations more useful for you?*', preempts that drift and signals that the mentor's ego is not more important than the mentee's development.

[66] Eby, L.T., Rhodes, J.E. & Allen, T.D. 2021. "Mentoring and developmental relationships in the workplace." *Annual Review of Organizational Psychology and Organizational Behavior 8*: 127–156.

Exercise: Where does your trust account stand?

Consider a current mentoring relationship. Rate yourself honestly on each dimension, not as you aspire to be, but as you are in practice.

- ☐ **Expertise**: Does your mentee have a clear and accurate sense of what you know and have experienced? Have you found natural opportunities to share your background without it feeling like a CV recitation?
- ☐ **Consistency**: Do you follow through on your commitments between sessions? Does your mentee know what to expect from you in terms of availability, responsiveness, and preparation?
- ☐ **Reliability**: When something comes up, a cancellation, a difficult piece of feedback, a situation you handled imperfectly, do you address it directly rather than hoping it passes unnoticed?
- ☐ **Authenticity:** Have you shared anything about your own struggles, mistakes, or uncertainties in a way that models the openness you are asking from your mentee?
- ☐ **Boundaries:** Have you been clear about what you can and cannot offer? Have you avoided overstepping into territory, personal, professional, or psychological, that is not yours to enter?
- ☐ **Receptiveness:** Have you asked your mentee how the relationship is working for them and responded without becoming defensive?

If any dimension produces a pause, a quiet recognition that you are not quite where you need to be, that is the most useful output of this exercise. Trust is not built by excelling on the dimensions you already find easy.

Conflicts of interest

Most mentors have at least one conflict of interest in at least one of their mentoring relationships. The conflict may be minor, a collegial friendship that makes complete honesty slightly awkward, or substantive, such as when a mentor directly influences a mentee's promotion. Either way, the professional response is acknowledgment, not avoidance.[67]

The reason avoidance fails is structural. An unacknowledged conflict of interest does not cease to influence the relationship; it simply does so beneath the surface, where neither party can examine it. The mentee may sense that certain topics elicit slightly different responses from the mentor but cannot name why. The mentor may find themselves subtly steering conversations away from territory that would expose the tension. Over time, these dynamics narrow the relationship without either party quite understanding why.

The table below outlines the most common types of conflict, how they manifest in practice, and how to handle them.

---

[67] Anderson, J. & Shannon, A. 2016. "The importance of confidentiality in mentoring." *Journal of Leadership Education 15,* no. 1: 224–232.

Type of conflict	What it looks like	How to handle it
Personal relationship	Mentor and mentee are friends, family members, or former close colleagues. The mentor may find it difficult to give an honest developmental challenge, or the mentee may resist feedback from someone they know socially.	Name it at the outset. Agree explicitly on how you will both signal when the personal relationship is influencing the professional one. Review it periodically.
Career stake	Mentor influences decisions on the mentee's pay, promotion, or continued employment, or stands to gain professionally if the mentee succeeds or fails.	Explicitly disclose the interest to the mentee and, where relevant, to program coordinators. Recuse yourself from decisions where the conflict is direct.
Competing loyalties	Mentor has close ties to a third party whose interests may diverge from the mentee's: for example, a mentor who is close to the mentee's line manager, or	Be transparent about the relationship. Avoid situations where information from the mentoring session might reach a third

Type of conflict	What it looks like	How to handle it
	who sits on the same leadership team.	party, even inadvertently.
Intellectual or professional overlap	Mentor and mentee work in the same niche, compete for the same clients or roles, or are involved in projects where the mentee's success affects the mentor's standing.	Consider whether the overlap is significant enough to preclude the relationship altogether. If not, agree on clear boundaries about what topics are and are not appropriate to discuss.

One principle applies across all of these: if you are uncertain whether a conflict of interest exists, that uncertainty is itself a reason to raise it. A transparent conversation about a possible conflict, *"I want to make sure we are both comfortable with how this is set up, given that I know your manager well"*, is unlikely to damage the relationship. A mentee discovering later that you concealed something is much more likely to.

Exercise: Confidentiality

The Confidentiality Conversation

Most mentors assume confidentiality is understood. Most mentees assume the same thing. Both assumptions, left unexamined, are a source of significant misunderstanding. Use the questions below to structure an explicit confidentiality conversation: ideally, in the first or second session, before you feel you need to have it.

For you to reflect on before the session:

- ☐ What am I prepared to keep completely confidential, and what circumstances, if any, would lead me to share something?
- ☐ Do I have any existing relationships with this mentee's manager, peers, or organization that could compromise my neutrality?
- ☐ If my organization has a formal mentoring program, what reporting obligations (if any) does it place on me?
- ☐ How would I handle a situation in which the mentee discloses something that concerns me seriously: personally, legally, or ethically?

Questions to raise with your mentee:

- ☐ "What does confidentiality mean to you in the context of our conversations? What would you want me to keep between us?"
- ☐ "Are there topics you would want to be careful about discussing, given our organizational context?"

- [ ] "If I ever heard something that genuinely concerned me, about your well-being or a situation involving others, how would you want me to handle that?"
- [ ] "Is there anything about our existing relationship or context that you think we should acknowledge before we start?"

This conversation does not need to be formal or lengthy. Done well, it takes ten minutes and transforms the psychological atmosphere of everything that follows. The point is not to draft a legal agreement. It is to make explicit what both parties assume and confirm that those assumptions align.

Debrief

'What is said in the room stays in the room' sounds obvious until you consider how rarely it is practiced, and how much the mentoring relationship depends on it. The point this chapter makes is not that confidentiality is a rule to be observed. Confidentiality is the structural condition that makes everything else in this book possible. Without it, the mentee self-censors, conversations stay safe, and the relationship realizes only a fraction of its potential.

The distinction between assumed and agreed confidentiality deserves particular attention. Most mentoring relationships skip the explicit conversation because both parties assume it is unnecessary. It is not. Assumptions that are never tested will eventually diverge, and when they do, the moment of discovery is rarely comfortable for either party.

The limits section reflects the uncomfortable reality that mentors operate within contexts of legal and ethical obligations that do not disappear simply because a conversation is designated as confidential. Knowing those limits before you need them, and being honest with mentees about their existence, is not a threat to the relationship. It is a mark of professionalism.

Trust, treated here as dynamic rather than fixed, asks something that most professional development does not: sustained attention to small behaviors over a long period. The mentor who consistently delivers on commitments, shares something genuine about their own experience, and asks how the relationship is working is building something that no single impressive session can replace. Trust is cumulative, directional, and fragile.

Your next step: If you have never had an explicit confidentiality conversation with a current mentee, schedule one in your next session, not as a formal agenda item, but as a natural check-in: '*I realize we have never talked about how we both think about confidentiality in our conversations. Can we take a few minutes to do that?*' You may be surprised by what surfaces. And if you have a potential conflict of interest that you have been quietly hoping would not become relevant, name it. Today is better than the moment it becomes relevant.

8. Mentoring and diversity

Bridging Differences Without Building Stereotypes

TL;DR

It would be simpler for mentors to believe they can treat everyone the same. The difference in a mentoring relationship is not a complication to be managed but a resource to be used, and mentors who understand this tend to be more useful to a wider range of people. Four dimensions get specific attention: gender, cultural background, generational difference, and values. Each shapes how a mentee experiences the relationship, what they feel safe saying, and whether the advice they receive fits their circumstances.

Benefitting from diversity

Every mentoring relationship involves two people who do not see the world in exactly the same way. That gap — managed well — is not a problem to be minimized. It is where much of the developmental value lives.

The evidence is unambiguous. Research from Cornell University found that mentoring increases retention and promotion rates for people from minority backgrounds by between 15% and 38%, compared with colleagues who were not mentored[68]. A separate study by the Association for Talent Development found that 44% of female CEOs identify mentoring programs as among the most important factors in their advancement to senior management[69]. These are not marginal effects. They suggest that access to good mentoring is one of the more consequential variables in whether talented people from underrepresented groups progress or plateau.

The implication for mentors is straightforward: the relationship works best when both parties bring genuinely different perspectives. A mentor who only feels comfortable working with people whose backgrounds mirror their own is not just limiting their mentee's development. They are limiting themselves.

Gender

Women in most professional environments still have less access to mentoring than their male counterparts, and the gap is most pronounced in male-dominated fields such as STEM[70]. The

---

[68] Conboy,K and Kelly,C 2016. What Evidence is There that Mentoring Works to Retain and Promote Employees, Especially Diverse Employees, Within a Single Company? Digital Collection @ILR. Cornell University. https://hdl.handle.net/1813/74541

[69] Kantor, K. 2018. Diversity + Mentoring = Increased Inclusion in the Workplace. October. *LinkedIn.* https://www.linkedin.com/pulse/diversity-mentoring-inclusion-julie-kantor/

[70] Powell, G. N., & Butterfield, D. A. 2013. Investigating the "glass ceiling" phenomenon: An empirical study of actual promotions to top management. *Academy of Management Journal* 36, no. 3: 593-613.

reasons are not mysterious: informal mentoring tends to follow existing social networks, and those networks have historically been built by and around men. The result is that talented women often navigate critical career junctures without the kind of experienced guidance that their male peers take for granted.

Structured mentoring programs can address this directly, and the evidence suggests they do. IBM's sponsorship initiative pairs high-potential women with senior executives who actively advocate for their careers — creating visibility and opening doors rather than simply offering advice[71]. IBM credits the program with measurable improvements in retention and advancement rates among women in the organization. Sheryl Sandberg's Lean In Circles take a different approach, building peer networks where women share experiences, develop skills, and mentor one another[72]. Both models share a common logic: access to developmental relationships does not happen by accident for people outside the dominant network; it must be deliberately created.

For individual mentors, the practical implication is worth sitting with. If your mentoring relationships are predominantly with people who share your gender, that is worth examining, not as a failing, but as a pattern that may be limiting both your impact and your own development.

---

[71].van Kralingen,B., Hunter, H., Chaney Reed,K., Baird,C. & Anderson,C. 2021. Women, leadership and missed opportunities. International Business Machines Corporation. https://www.ibm.com/downloads/cas/3ZNDMAPE

[72] Sandberg, S. 2013. *Lean in: Women, Work, and the Will to Lead.* Random House.
LeanIn.org. 2021. *Lean In Circles*. https://leanin.org/circles

Cultural diversity

Cultural background shapes how people communicate, how they interpret feedback, what they expect from a relationship with a more senior colleague, and what professional success means to them. A mentor who assumes these things are universal is not being culturally insensitive in any dramatic sense. They are simply working from an incomplete picture, and the advice they give will reflect that incompleteness[73].

Cross-cultural mentoring pairs, where mentor and mentee come from genuinely different cultural backgrounds, can be among the most productive relationships precisely because neither party can rely on shared assumptions. Everything has to be made explicit: what the mentee is hoping for, what the mentor is offering, and what each of them means by the words they are using. That process of making the implicit explicit tends to produce more honest and more useful conversations than relationships where both parties assume they already understand each other[74].

Affinity groups and peer networks built around shared cultural identity serve a different but complementary purpose. They provide a space where people can speak candidly about experiences that a cross-cultural mentor may not fully grasp, and where mentoring can happen between people at similar career stages who face similar structural challenges. Neither model is

---

[73] Okoroji, C. 2017. "Mentoring in culturally diverse settings: A systematic review." *Journal of International Education and Practice* 1, no. 2: 107-115.

[74] Blake-Beard, S., Bayne, M. L., Crosby, F. J., & Muller, C. B. 2015. "Matching by race and gender in mentoring relationships: Keeping our eyes on the prize." *Journal of Social Issues* 71, no. 3: 468-482.

superior. They address different needs, and the most well-supported professionals tend to have access to both.

The practical question for any mentor is simply this: how much do you know about the cultural context your mentee is operating from, and how often do you check your assumptions rather than acting on them?[75]

Generational

Generational difference is probably the most visible form of diversity in most mentoring relationships, and also the most likely to be underestimated. The gap between a mentor in their fifties and a mentee in their late twenties is not just a difference in experience. It is a difference in the working world each of them grew up in: different assumptions about hierarchy and authority, different relationships with technology, different expectations about what a career is supposed to look like, and how fast it is supposed to move.

The traditional model assumes that knowledge flows in one direction, from the more experienced person to the less experienced one. In cross-generational relationships, that assumption needs to be examined. A mentor who is genuinely curious about how their mentee navigates a world shaped by social media, remote work, and AI tools will learn things they cannot get anywhere else[76]. This is the logic behind reverse mentoring, as discussed in Chapter 3, and it applies, in some measure, to every

---

[75] Zikic,J 2016. "When Mentorship Crosses Cultures, Both Sides Learn." *Harvard Business Review.* August.

[76] Satterly, B.A., Cullen, J. and Dyson, D.A. 2018. "The intergenerational mentoring model: an alternative to traditional and reverse models of mentoring." *Mentoring & Tutoring: Partnership in Learning* 26, no. 4: 441-454.

mentoring relationship that crosses a significant generational gap.

What makes generational difference productive rather than merely awkward is the same thing that makes any form of difference productive: acknowledging it directly rather than pretending it is not there. A mentor who says, "*I'm aware that the career path I took probably looks quite different from the options you're weighing,* " opens a more honest conversation than one who assumes their own experience is a reliable map for someone twenty-five years younger. The gap is an asset. It just needs to be named.

Values

Every mentoring conversation is shaped by values that neither party has necessarily examined or declared. What one person means by ambition, success, loyalty, or work-life balance is not universal. It is the product of their background, family, culture, and experience. When a mentor and mentee share similar values, conversations tend to feel easy and natural. When they do not, something subtler happens: advice that seems entirely reasonable to the mentor can land as tone-deaf to the mentee, without either party understanding why.

The Valuegraphics research identifies the ten most commonly held values across cultures[77]. It is worth spending a moment with this list before your next mentoring session, not to categorize your mentee, but to prompt a useful question: which of these do I hold most strongly, and how might that shape the guidance I give to someone whose priorities look different from

---

[77] The World's Most Influential Values, in One Graphic. https://www.visualcapitalist.com/most-influential-values/

mine?

1	Family
2	Relationships
3	Financial security
4	Belonging
5	Community
6	Personal growth
7	Loyalty
8	Spirituality
9	Job security
10	Personal responsibility

Source: https://www.visualcapitalist.com/most-influential-values/

The more interesting insight from the research is that excessive similarity in values can be as limiting as excessive difference. A mentor and mentee who share identical priorities tend to reinforce each other's existing assumptions rather than challenge them. The mentee leaves each session feeling understood but not stretched. Some productive friction, the kind that comes from genuinely different perspectives on what matters, is not a problem to be smoothed over. It is part of what makes the relationship worth having.

A brief, early conversation about values need not be formal or philosophical. Something as simple as "*I've found that people mean quite different things by work-life balance or career success — it would help me to understand what those things mean to you*" surfaces the relevant differences without making the relationship feel like a sociology seminar.

Exercise: The assumption audit

Most mentors give advice in good faith based on what worked for them. The problem is that what worked for you, in your context, with your background and your networks, may not translate directly to someone whose circumstances are meaningfully different. This exercise is designed to make that gap visible.

Part 1: Looking back

Think of a recent conversation where you gave a mentee advice or guidance. Work through the questions below honestly, with that specific conversation in mind.

- Did you assume your mentee had access to the same networks, resources, or opportunities that were available to you at a similar stage?
- Did you factor in constraints that may not apply to you, such as financial pressures, visa status, family expectations, or caregiving responsibilities?
- Did you assume that "professional behavior, " "ambition, " or "success" mean the same thing in your mentee's context as they do in yours?
- Did you assume your mentee had the same level of organizational knowledge or political awareness that you had accumulated by their career stage?

If any of those questions gave you pause, that is useful information. It does not mean the advice you gave was wrong. It means the advice may have needed to be adapted to fit your mentee's circumstances, and making that adjustment is your job, not theirs.

Part 2: Looking forward

Before your next mentoring session, consider building one of the following questions into the conversation:

- "I want to make sure the suggestions I make actually fit your situation. What constraints or considerations should I understand before I offer a view?"
- "My experience of this was shaped by a particular set of circumstances. How does your situation differ from that?"
- "What would make my advice genuinely useful to you, rather than just relevant to someone in my position?"

You do not need to use all three. Use the one that you feel fits the situation. Asking sincerely and following up is worth more than a checklist completed perfunctorily.

Part 3: Your commitment

Write one thing you will do differently in your next mentoring conversation based on what this exercise has surfaced.

Debrief

The four dimensions covered in this chapter, gender, cultural background, generational difference, and values, are not separate problems requiring separate solutions. They are different expressions of the same underlying challenge: the mentor who can only work effectively with people who share their background, outlook, and career experience is operating with a significantly reduced range. That limits their mentees. It also limits them.

The evidence on outcomes is worth restating plainly. Mentored individuals from minority backgrounds have retention and promotion rates that are 15 to 38 percentage points higher than those without mentors. Access to good mentoring is not a nice-to-have in someone's career. For many people, it is the difference between progressing and plateauing.

The values section deserves particular attention on reflection. The Valuegraphics list is not an academic exercise. It is a practical prompt for a conversation most mentoring relationships never have. When a mentor and mentee find themselves talking past each other, or when advice that seems entirely sensible goes unacted upon, a difference in underlying values is often part of the explanation.

Which brings us to the line worth carrying from this chapter: your advice needs to fit your mentee's circumstances, not just your own experience of similar ones. The mentor who grasps that distinction and acts on it is considerably more useful than one who dispenses wisdom on the assumption that what worked for them will work for everyone.

Your next step: Before your next mentoring session, work through the values table yourself and rank the ten values in order of personal importance. Then ask your mentee to do the same and compare notes openly. The differences are not awkward. They are the point.

9. Mentoring toolbox

When Your Questions Matter More Than Your Answers

TL;DR

Personality attributes tell you who to be as a mentor; techniques tell you what to do. This chapter explores four approaches that turn good intentions into genuine impact: Socratic questioning, the GROW model, storytelling, and role modeling. Socrates understood 2,400 years ago what modern research confirms: people learn more from wrestling with questions than from receiving answers. The GROW model gives questioning a practical structure, moving from Goal to Reality to Options to Will. The Five Whys technique takes you deeper when surface answers are not enough. Storytelling and role modeling round out the toolkit.

Developing your mentoring toolbox

If you have ever opened your toolbox at home, you will recognize a familiar pattern: it is crammed with dozens of tools accumulated over the years, yet when you need to hang a picture or fix a wobbly chair, you reach for the same five favorites every time. The other tools sit there gathering dust until that one awkward job comes along that absolutely requires the pipe wrench you bought three years ago and forgot you owned.

Your mentoring practice works the same way. Most mentors develop preferred techniques: approaches that feel comfortable, align with their personality, and have worked well in the past. There is nothing wrong with having favorites. The challenge is recognizing when your go-to approach is not quite right for the situation at hand. Your favorite Socratic questioning style works brilliantly when a mentee needs to think through a complex decision, but it can feel frustratingly indirect when they need concrete guidance about organizational politics. Your storytelling captivates mentees who learn through narrative, yet leaves others impatient for practical frameworks.

This is why effective mentors maintain that messy, overstuffed toolbox, not because they will use every technique in every conversation, but because they have developed the judgment to recognize which tool the moment requires. The four techniques in this chapter, Socratic questioning, the GROW model, storytelling, and role modeling, are your hammer, screwdriver, wrench, and measuring tape: versatile, broadly applicable, and worth mastering. You will likely find one or two resonate more naturally with your style. Develop those until they become second nature, but keep the others sharp, because the mentee who arrives next month may need something entirely different from what worked last week.

Socratic questioning

Tracing its roots to Socrates, Socratic questioning guides mentees to explore their own thought processes rather than receive ready-made answers. The mentor poses thought-provoking, open-ended questions that challenge assumptions and prompt critical thinking, while actively listening and allowing the mentee to explore ideas freely.[78]

Effective Socratic questioning has four components. **Clarification**: questions that help both parties get to the same understanding of what is being discussed. **Probing assumptions**, identifying and challenging beliefs the mentee holds that may limit their perspective, encouraging them to present evidence and evaluate whether those beliefs hold up. **Encouraging alternate viewpoints**, introducing different perspectives, and prompting the mentee to question their own biases. **Exploring implications and consequences**, helping the mentee think through the potential outcomes of their decisions and whether those outcomes are ones they can live with.

In practice, assume your mentee is struggling with an important work-related decision. Each component suggests a different kind of question:

Clarification: "*When you say this decision feels risky, what specifically are you worried about: the outcome itself, or what others will think if it goes wrong?*"

---

[78]Paul, Richard, and Linda Elder. 2019. *The Miniature Guide to Critical Thinking Concepts and Tools*, 8th ed. Lanham, MD: Rowman & Littlefield.

Probing assumptions: "*What is telling you that is the right call: is that based on data, gut feel, or what worked last time?*"

Alternate viewpoints: "*You have described this as a choice between X and Y, but what if that's not the choice you're facing?*"

Implications: *"If you went with that option and it didn't work out the way you're hoping, what would that mean for you, and could you live with it?*"

A framework for effective questioning

Socratic questioning gives you a set of principles. The GROW model gives you a structure to put them into practice. Developed by Sir John Whitmore and colleagues in the late 1980s, GROW has become the standard framework in coaching and mentoring because it provides just enough structure to keep conversations productive while leaving room for the improvisation that effective mentoring requires.[79]

The acronym stands for Goal, Reality, Options, and Will, four stages that mirror how we naturally approach any problem when we are thinking clearly. When your mentee is stressed, overwhelmed, or stuck, clear thinking is precisely what deserts them. That is where a mentor with a questioning framework becomes valuable.

Think of GROW as a map for your mentoring conversation, not a script. You might spend five minutes in one stage and twenty in another. You might loop back to Reality after exploring

---

[79]Whitmore, John. 2017. Coaching for Performance: The Principles and Practice of Coaching and Leadership, 5th ed. London: Nicholas Brealey Publishing.

Options. That is fine, you are improvising within a structure, like a jazz musician working with chord changes.

Goal: Where do you want to be?

Start by establishing what your mentee wants to achieve, not just in general, but specifically from this conversation. It is surprising how often we dive into problem-solving without clearly defining what 'solved' looks like. Sometimes the goal is clear ("*I need to decide whether to apply for this promotion*"); sometimes it is vague ("*I'm just feeling a bit stuck*"). Both are fine. If it is fuzzy, spend longer here.

> *"What would you like to focus on today?"*
>
> *"What would success look like?"*
>
> *"If we have a really productive conversation, what will be different when you leave?"*

Reality: Where are you now?

Help your mentee map their current situation. Your job is not to solve anything yet. It is to help them see clearly. This stage often takes the longest because assumptions surface, blind spots emerge, and the real issue (as opposed to the presenting issue) comes to light.

> *"What have you tried already?"*
>
> *"Who else is involved or affected?"*
>
> *"On a scale of 1–10, how challenging does this feel right now?"*
>
> *"What's already working, even partially?"*

Options: What could you do?

Only now, once the goal is clear and reality is mapped, do you explore possibilities. Notice the plural, options, not option. Your job is to help your mentee generate multiple possibilities, even if they are imperfect or unlikely. This is where you can share your own experiences, but frame them as additional options rather than prescriptions.

"What options do you have?"

"If you had unlimited resources, what would you do?"

"What would you advise a colleague in this situation?"

"What would happen if you did nothing?"

Will: What will you do?

This is where insight becomes action. Your mentee has explored the territory, identified possibilities, and is now committed to a specific path forward. Notice the shift from 'could' to 'will.' If the commitment sounds half-hearted, go back to Options; a reluctant "*I suppose I could try...*" is not a plan. The conversation should end with specific commitments, ideally written down: not "*I'll think about it*" but "*I will speak with Sarah on Tuesday morning before the team meeting.*"

"Which option will you pursue?"

"What's your first step, and when exactly will you do it?"

"On a scale of 1–10, how committed are you to this action?"

GROW in action

Mentee: *I'm thinking about whether to apply for the regional manager role.*

Mentor (Goal): *Let's explore that. What would you like to get out of* *our conversation today: are you deciding whether to apply, or something else?*

Mentee: *I think I want to apply, but I'm not sure I'm ready. So, I guess I want to figure out if I should go for it now or wait.*

Mentor (Reality): *What makes you uncertain about your readiness?*

Mentee: *Well, I've only been in this role for 18 months, and the job description requires 3 years' minimum...*

Mentor (Reality): *And what's underneath that concern?*

Mentee: *I suppose I'm worried I'll look presumptuous. Like I'm overreaching.*

Mentor (Options): *So, you've identified three possible paths: apply now, wait six months, or talk to the hiring manager before deciding. What else might you do?*

Mentee: *I suppose I could talk to Maria, she made a similar move last year...*

Mentor (Will): *Which path are you going to take?*

Mentee: *I'm going to speak with Maria this week, then with the hiring manager next week, and make my decision after that.*

Mentor (Will): *Good. What day will you contact Maria?*

Mentee: *Thursday.*

Notice how the mentor did not tell the mentee what to do but used questions to help them think through their situation systematically. The mentee left with their own decision and clear next steps.

When GROW does not work

GROW is designed for problem-solving and decision-making conversations. Do not force it when your mentee needs information or technical knowledge (just share it), when they need emotional support rather than action planning (listen first), when they are processing a setback (reflection before action), or when the conversation is genuinely exploratory with no specific goal. Remember: you are a skilled improviser, not a robot following a script. GROW is a tool in your toolbox, not a straitjacket.

Exercise: Identifying GROW stages

Read these mentor questions and identify which GROW stage each belongs to:

	Question	Stage
1.	"What's your ultimate objective with this project?"	
2.	"What resources do you already have available?"	
3.	"What would happen if you delegated this task?"	
4.	"When specifically will you have that conversation?"	
5.	"What's stopping you from moving forward?"	
6.	"If you had no constraints, what would you do?"	
7.	"How committed are you to this approach?"	
8.	"What have you tried so far?"	

Try this yourself: in your next mentoring conversation, note which GROW stage you are in as you progress. You will likely discover you have a preference, perhaps you are good at exploring Reality but rush through Options, or the reverse. That is your improvisation edge, the place where developing your flexibility will pay off most.

Root cause analysis: Five Whys

When a mentee gives you a surface-level answer, the Five Whys technique takes you deeper. Originally developed by Taiichi Ohno at Toyota as a manufacturing problem-solving method, it works just as well in a mentoring conversation.[80] The approach is simple: when a mentee describes a problem, ask "why is that?" or "what's underneath that?" up to five times, with each question peeling back another layer. Be careful not to sound like a prosecuting barrister: your tone needs to convey genuine curiosity, not interrogation.

Five Whys in action

Sarah, a mid-level project manager, meets with her mentor, David. She is clearly stressed.

Sarah: *I'm drowning. I've got three major projects running simultaneously, and I can't keep up. I'm working 60-hour weeks and still falling behind.*

David: *That sounds exhausting. Help me understand,* ***why*** *are you falling behind despite putting in all those hours?*

Sarah: *Because there's just too much work. Every project has unrealistic deadlines, and I'm the only one who can handle the complexity.*

David: *Okay, so you're the only one managing these complex projects.* ***Why*** *is that?*

Sarah: *My team doesn't have the experience yet. When things get complicated, they come to me. I end up redoing their work or just doing it myself from the start.*

---

[80]Ohno, Taiichi. 1988. *Toyota Production System: Beyond Large-Scale Production*. Portland, OR: Productivity Press.

David: *So, your team comes to you when things get complicated.* ***Why*** *don't they handle those situations themselves?*

Sarah: (pauses) *I suppose... perhaps I have never really given them the chance? When something's urgent, it's faster if I just do it. And honestly, I worry they'll make mistakes that I'll have to fix anyway.*

David: *So you handle the complex work because you're concerned about mistakes.* **Why** *does the possibility of mistakes feel like such a problem?*

Sarah: (longer pause) *Because... if they mess up, it reflects badly on me. My manager will think I can't lead the team properly. I'm up for promotion next quarter, and I need everything to run perfectly.*

David: *So you're protecting your promotion prospects by personally handling the complex work.* **Why** *does that strategy feel like the safest path?*

Sarah: (sits back) *When you put it that way... it doesn't sound safe at all, does it? I'm burning out, my team isn't developing, and I'm creating a situation where I'm indispensable to day-to-day operations. That's not what senior managers do. I'm undermining my promotion by trying too hard to protect it.*

Five questions. The presenting problem ("too much work") turned out to be a fear of delegation driven by promotion anxiety. The mentor did not diagnose this; the mentee discovered it herself, which means she is far more likely to act on it.

Storytelling

Storytelling is one of the oldest teaching methods and one of the most effective. Research on knowledge transfer in organizations has found that stories are retained more accurately and for longer than abstract principles, because narrative engages both the brain's analytical and emotional processing systems.[81] A mentor who says "*resilience matters*" is giving advice. A mentor who describes the moment their startup nearly went under, the funding that fell through, the difficult conversation with their co-founder, the moment they nearly walked away, is giving their mentee something they will remember years later.

Storytelling in mentoring takes two forms:

Personal experience, sharing your own successes, failures, and turning points, works because it is authentic and specific. It also signals vulnerability, which builds trust. The risk is making the conversation about you rather than your mentee, so keep the story focused on the lesson, not the autobiography.

Anecdotal examples, stories about other people, public figures, or situations you have observed, provide useful distance when direct experience might feel too personal or prescriptive. They also widen the range of experiences you can draw on. A mentor who has never changed careers can still share a well-chosen story about someone who did.

The key to both forms is that a story without a question afterwards is just an anecdote. The value lies in what your mentee does with it. "*What struck you about that?*" or "*Does any of that resonate with what you're facing?*" turns a story into a learning moment.

---

[81]Swap, Walter, Dorothy Leonard, Mimi Shields, and Lisa Abrams. 2001. "Using Mentoring and Storytelling to Transfer Knowledge in the Workplace." *Journal of Management Information Systems* 18, no. 1: 95–114.

Role modeling

Role modeling is the mentoring technique that requires the fewest words and the most self-awareness. Every time you interact with your mentee, you are demonstrating how a senior professional behaves, whether you intend to or not. How you prepare for meetings, how you respond to unexpected bad news, how you treat the most junior person in the room, how you handle being wrong, all of it is observed, processed, and often imitated.

Deliberate role modeling means being conscious of this and using it. When you openly admit you do not understand a new system and ask your mentee to walk you through it, you are demonstrating that senior professionals do not need to know everything. When you describe how you handled a difficult conversation with a colleague, including what you got wrong, you are showing that self-reflection is part of the job, not a sign of weakness. When you set boundaries around your own working hours, you are giving your mentee permission to do the same.

The trap is assuming that role modeling means projecting an image of competence. It does not. It means being honest about how you work, including the messy, uncertain, and still-in-progress parts. Your mentee does not need a role model who appears to have everything figured out. They need one who demonstrates that figuring it out is an ongoing process.

Debrief

Most mentors instinctively default to advice-giving because it feels helpful and efficient. You have solved this problem before; why not just tell your mentee the answer? Because people retain a fraction of what they are told but a great deal of what they work out for themselves. That is why these techniques matter.

Socratic questioning hands your mentee a mirror, not a map. The GROW model provides structure to questioning without turning it into a script. The Five Whys technique reveals the real issue hiding beneath the presenting one. Storytelling lodges lessons in memory far more effectively than abstract advice. And role modeling, the most potent technique of all, requires no words, only the willingness to let your mentee see how you operate rather than how you think you should.

There is a fifth set of tools that deserves mention here, though it sits slightly apart from the others. Throughout this book, the skilled improviser has served as a metaphor for what effective mentoring looks like in practice: prepared but responsive, structured but adaptive. That metaphor draws on a real discipline with real techniques. Improvisation, not the comedic performance variety, but the collaborative, generative methodology that underpins it, offers a set of practical exercises that develop precisely the skills this chapter has been building: active listening, presence, the ability to build on what your mentee offers rather than redirecting it, and comfort with not knowing what comes next. Appendix C provides a short toolkit of these exercises, adapted specifically for mentoring conversations. If the techniques in this chapter tell you what to do, the improviser's toolkit helps you practice how to be while you are doing it.

Your next step: Review your last mentoring conversation. Did you tell more than you asked? Next time, try reversing the ratio, ask three questions for every piece of advice you offer. Notice what happens when your mentee thinks instead of you.

10. Mentorship malpractice

The warning signs you shouldn't ignore

TL;DR

Every mentoring book should include this chapter, yet most do not, perhaps because acknowledging that mentoring can go badly wrong undermines the feel-good narrative. But the evidence demands attention: more than half of mentees in workplace settings report at least one negative mentoring experience, and the effects of poor mentoring can be more damaging than having no mentor at all. This chapter helps you distinguish among five categories of negative mentoring experiences, recognize early warning signs, and understand what both mentors and organizations can do to prevent problems before they start. Uncomfortable reading? Absolutely. Essential? Even more so.

Why this chapter matters

Most forms of mentoring involve an interaction between individuals at different levels of seniority and power. Given this potential imbalance, mentors should be alert to situations that do not contribute directly, transparently, and ethically to a mentee's development. The assumption that mentoring is always positive, that simply having a mentor is better than not having one, does not withstand scrutiny, considering the evidence. Research has consistently shown that negative mentoring experiences can leave mentees worse off than those without a mentor, leading to increased stress, reduced job satisfaction, psychological withdrawal from work, and higher turnover intention.[82]

This is not a fringe finding. In their widely cited taxonomy of negative mentoring, Eby and colleagues found that more than 50% of workplace mentees reported at least one negative experience with their mentor. These experiences ranged from relatively mild (a mismatch of working styles or a mentor who lacked the relevant expertise) to serious and deliberate (manipulation, credit-taking, and sabotage). More recent work has confirmed that the problem persists across different organizational and cultural contexts, and that even infrequent negative experiences can have disproportionately strong effects on the mentee's well-being and performance.[83]

---

[82] Hu, Zhonghui, Jinsong Li, and Ho Kwong Kwan. "The Effects of Negative Mentoring Experiences on Mentor Creativity: The Roles of Mentor Ego Depletion and Traditionality." *Human Resource Management* 61, no. 1 (2022): 39–54

[83] Hu, Zhonghui, Ho Kwong Kwan, Yingying Zhang, and Jinsong Li. "The Effects of Negative Mentoring Experiences on Protégés' Turnover Intention: The Roles of Harmonious Work Passion and

The chapter that follows is not about bad people. Most mentors who cause harm do not intend to. They are busy, under-trained, unaware of their blind spots, or simply operating with good intentions and poor skills. That is precisely why understanding what can go wrong matters: it is the well-meaning mentor, not the overtly abusive one, who is most likely to cause damage without realizing it.

The spectrum of negative mentoring

Mentoring malpractice is not a single phenomenon. It exists on a continuum, and understanding where specific problems sit on that continuum helps determine the appropriate response. Five broad categories capture most of what goes wrong in mentoring relationships.

The first is a mismatch within the pair. This involves incompatible working styles, clashing values, or fundamentally different assumptions about the relationship's purpose. Neither party is behaving badly; they simply don't work well together. This is the most common source of difficulty and often the easiest to address if someone names it early enough.

The second is distancing behavior. The mentor becomes unavailable, cancels meetings, responds slowly to messages, or becomes emotionally disengaged. This is rarely a conscious decision. It is the product of competing priorities, declining interest, or a growing sense that the relationship is not working, expressed through withdrawal rather than conversation. The mentee experiences neglect, even though the mentor may simply feel overcommitted.

Moqi with the Mentor." *Journal of Managerial Psychology* 39, no. 6 (2024): 716–31. https://doi.org/10.1108/JMP-01-2023-0017.

The third is manipulative behavior. This includes a mentor taking credit for the mentee's work, using the mentee's connections for personal advancement, assigning work that serves the mentor's interests rather than the mentee's development, or creating a dependency that serves the mentor's need to feel valued rather than the mentee's need to grow. This category is less common than the first two but considerably more damaging.

The fourth is a lack of expertise. The mentor may lack the technical knowledge, industry experience, or interpersonal skills to be genuinely helpful. They may offer advice confidently on subjects they do not understand well, or they may fail to recognize the limits of their own experience. A mentor whose career peaked in a different era yet offers definitive guidance on today's job market is a familiar example.

The fifth is general dysfunction. This covers mentors whose personal problems, negative attitudes, or erratic behavior create an unstable or toxic dynamic. It also includes situations where the mentor uses the relationship to process their own frustrations, treating the mentee as a sounding board for grievances rather than providing developmental support.

These categories are not mutually exclusive, and they are not always visible to the mentor. A mentor who is simultaneously too busy to meet regularly (distancing) and prone to offering authoritative advice on topics outside their expertise (lack of expertise) may believe they are being helpful during the sessions that do occur. The mentee, meanwhile, experiences an unreliable relationship in which the advice they do receive is questionable - a combination that erodes trust faster than either problem would on its own.

The impact on mentors

An important and often overlooked dimension of negative mentoring is the toll it takes on the mentor. The literature has traditionally focused on the mentee as the party at risk, and for good reason; they hold less power in the relationship. But Hu, Li, and Kwan (2022) found that negative mentoring experiences significantly depleted mentors' self-regulatory resources, leading to reduced creativity and increased emotional exhaustion. Mentoring that goes badly is draining for everyone involved, and a depleted mentor is less able to serve their mentees, their team, and their own development.

This finding matters in practice because it challenges the assumption that mentors can simply absorb difficult relationships at no cost. A mentor who persists with a dysfunctional mentoring relationship out of obligation or guilt is not being virtuous; they are depleting resources that could be better invested elsewhere. Recognizing this is not selfish; it is responsible.

Early warning signs

All relationships, even mentoring ones, can be tricky to maintain at times. Problems rarely announce themselves with a single dramatic incident. They accumulate through a series of small signals that are easy to dismiss individually but form a clear pattern when viewed together. One useful diagnostic framework, originally developed in a medical education context, identifies six 'extremes' of mentee behavior that can indicate emerging difficulties within a mentoring relationship.

The overstretched mentee takes on more commitments than they can manage, consistently arrives unprepared, and treats mentoring sessions as one more obligation to survive rather than an opportunity to develop. The disappearing mentee frequently cancels, responds to messages with long delays, and allows the intervals between meetings to stretch until the relationship effectively lapses. The over-submissive mentee agrees with everything the mentor says, never pushes back or offers an alternative view, and treats the mentor's suggestions as instructions to follow rather than ideas to discuss.

The over-dependent mentee contacts the mentor excessively between sessions, struggles to make decisions without the mentor's input, and shows little sign of developing the autonomy that mentoring is supposed to build. The individualistic mentee rejects collaboration, ignores the mentor's advice, and treats the partnership as a formality instead of an opportunity for growth. The untrustworthy mentee misrepresents what happened in previous sessions, shares confidential information outside the relationship, or fails to follow through on agreed actions without acknowledging it.

These are not character judgments. They are diagnostic patterns that indicate when a relationship needs attention. A mentee who is overly submissive may simply be intimidated by the mentor's seniority; one who disappears may be struggling with problems they haven't felt safe disclosing. The mentor's job is to notice the pattern and address it directly: "*I've noticed that you tend to agree with whatever I suggest, I'd much rather hear when you think I'm wrong*" opens a conversation that silence never will.

What can organizations do?

Individual mentors can prevent many problems through awareness and skill, but the organizational context matters too. A mentoring program that pairs people together, provides no training, offers no oversight, and has no mechanism for raising concerns is creating the conditions in which malpractice can thrive unchecked. Treasure et al. (2022) set out ten principles for establishing effective mentoring programs, emphasizing that sustainable programs require defined guidelines, trained mentors, regular evaluation, and accessible reporting mechanisms: not as bureaucratic additions, but as the infrastructure that keeps relationships healthy.[84]

Six measures deserve attention.

1. E**stablish clear guidelines for mentoring relationship**s, including boundaries, expectations, and what constitutes acceptable and unacceptable behavior.
2. Encourage mentors and mentees to discuss potential conflicts of interest at the outset and agree on how to handle them.
3. **Provide training or support to equip mentors** with the knowledge and skills to be effective: Chapter 11 covers this in detail.
4. **Create a safe reporting mechanism** so that mentees and mentors can raise concerns without fear of retaliation.
5. **Schedule regular check-ins with both parties** to ensure the relationship remains healthy and productive.
6. Hold both mentors and mentees accountable for their conduct and take appropriate action when problems are reported.

These measures are not bureaucratic box-ticking. They are the infrastructure that prevents good intentions from sliding into exploitation. Without them, mentors who believe they are "just

---

[84] Treasure, Anne M., Siobhan Mackenzie Hall, Igor Lesko, Derek Moore, Malvika Sharan, Menno van Zaanen, Yo Yehudi, and Anelda van der Walt. "Ten Simple Rules for Establishing a Mentorship Program." *PLOS Computational Biology* 18, no. 5 (2022): e1010015. https://doi.org/10.1371/journal.pcbi.1010015.

helping" may exploit mentees' connections for personal advancement or withhold opportunities to maintain control, and neither party may recognize what is happening until the damage is done.

Exercise: The mentoring health check

This exercise is designed to be completed periodically, every three to four months, as a quick diagnostic of your mentoring relationship. Answer honestly; the exercise is for your own reflection, not for sharing with your mentee (though discussing the themes that emerge may well be valuable).

For each statement, rate yourself on a scale of 1 (strongly disagree) to 5 (strongly agree):	
1. My mentee appears comfortable disagreeing with me or offering a different perspective.	
2. Our meetings happen at the agreed frequency, and neither of us routinely reschedules.	
3. My mentee is making decisions and taking actions independently, rather than waiting for my approval.	
4. I am confident that the advice I give is within my area of genuine expertise.	
5. I have asked my mentee for feedback on how the relationship is working, and genuinely listened to the an-	
6. I can identify specific ways in which my mentee has developed since we started working together.	
7. I am learning something from this relationship, not just giving.	
8. If my mentee had a concern about my behavior, I believe they would feel safe raising it with me.	
Total	

Scoring: A total of 32–40 suggests a healthy relationship. 24–31 indicates areas worth discussing with your mentee. A score below 24 suggests the relationship needs direct attention, and possibly a frank conversation about whether it is serving either party well.

Pay particular attention to any individual item scored at 1 or 2. A single low score may point to a specific issue that can be addressed; several low scores together suggest a more systemic problem. The items are deliberately weighted toward the mentee's experience and autonomy, because that is where problems are most likely to go unnoticed by the mentor.

Debrief

If more than half of mentees report at least one negative mentoring experience, and if bad mentoring can leave people worse off than no mentoring at all, then the feel-good assumption that mentoring is inherently beneficial deserves serious qualification. The power imbalance in most mentoring relationships creates vulnerability that well-meaning mentors can exploit without intending harm, and the damage extends in both directions, depleting the mentor's own resources and the mentee's confidence.

The five categories of negative mentoring experience, mismatch, distancing, manipulation, lack of expertise, and general dysfunction, are diagnostic tools, not character judgments. The same applies to the six early warning patterns. Spotting these signs early means addressing problems while they are still fixable, rather than waiting for the relationship to collapse or simply allowing it to fade into mutual avoidance.

The six organizational measures outlined in this chapter, clear guidelines, conflict-of-interest discussions, mentor training, safe reporting, regular check-ins, and genuine accountability, are not optional extras. They are the differences between mentoring programs that develop people and those that occasionally damage them.

Your next step: Complete the mentoring health check. If you score below 24, or if any single item is 1 or 2, schedule a conversation with your mentee about what you're observing. If your organization's mentoring program doesn't have all six measures in place, closing that gap isn't difficult; it's responsible. Early intervention prevents later disasters.

11. Organizing a mentoring program

Turning mentoring from a nice idea into an organizational culture

TL;DR:

Most organizations launch mentoring programs with enthusiasm and good intentions, then wonder why they fizzle within months. This chapter provides the unglamorous infrastructure that separates sustainable programs from expensive failures. You will discover five organizational objectives that mentoring can genuinely address, but only with proper design. The needs analysis section covers four critical stages: defining objectives, identifying target audiences, conducting skill gap analysis, and making successful matches. Mentor training is not optional; seven key components ensure mentors know what they are doing.

Purpose & objectives

When companies embark on an in-house mentoring program, their goals should align with recognizable organizational objectives. Here are some typical objectives they may wish to address[85]:

1. **Talent Development and Retention.** Mentorship programs should aim to cultivate talent within an organization by giving employees access to more experienced colleagues, enabling them to learn, develop new skills and perspectives, and explore career options. This can result in increased employee engagement, job satisfaction, and loyalty within your workforce.
2. **Knowledge Transfer**. Mentorship programs can also promote internal knowledge transfer, with experienced mentors sharing industry know-how with mentees to maximize knowledge transfer and skill acquisition. By sharing expertise within an in-house mentoring program, more knowledgeable employees may become available, providing your workforce with greater expertise.
3. **Diversity and Inclusion**. Mentorship programs can also promote diversity and inclusion by pairing employees from diverse backgrounds, genders, or ethnicities to encourage cross-cultural understanding and break down barriers.
4. **Succession Planning**. In-house mentoring programs can assist companies with succession planning by identifying high-potential employees and offering mentoring and

---

[85] Gartner. 2019. *Develop a Successful Mentoring Program by Defining Objectives and Metrics*. From: https://www.gartner.com/smarterwithgartner/develop-a-successful-mentoring-program-by-defining-objectives-and-metrics/

development opportunities that nurture future leaders within their company.

5. **Employee Engagement**. Mentoring can contribute to employee engagement by giving employees a sense of purpose and opportunities for career growth, leading to higher job satisfaction and retention.

Proof of benefits

Although it is notoriously challenging to determine the cause and impact of mentoring upon an organization, there has been no lack of effort in this field! The Association for Talent Development demonstrated that organizations with mentoring programs had higher employee retention and were more likely to report that employees were highly engaged.[86] Another study conducted by the Society for Human Resource Management discovered that mentoring programs are effective tools in developing future leaders while simultaneously increasing diversity and inclusion[87].

Needs analysis

Needs analysis is the foundation of an effective in-house mentoring program. It should clarify the skills, knowledge, and behaviors mentees are expected to acquire, as well as the benefits mentees gain from the mentors' expertise and experience.

---

[86] Association for Talent Development. 2015. *Mentoring Matters*. https://www.td.org/research-reports/mentoring-matters

[87] Society for Human Resource Management. 2019. *Mentoring and Coaching: Developing the Next Generation of Leaders*. https://www.shrm.org/hr-today/trends-and-forecasting/research-and-surveys/Documents/Mentoring%20and%20Coaching%20Developing%20the%20Next%20Generation%20of%20Leaders.pdf

Although the approach can vary widely, it often involves several similar stages.

1. **Program objectives**. The initial step in needs analysis is to define the goals and objectives for any mentoring program, including specific skills, knowledge, or behaviors intended to be improved or developed through the program, such as leadership capabilities, technical expertise, or career advancement.
2. **Target audience.** Early in the process, it is important to identify the attributes of the typical mentee candidates. This involves determining who stands to gain most from participating and who has most to contribute as mentors. Potential target groups could include employees at specific levels within an organization, departments, or people with specific skill sets who could contribute to mentorship roles.
3. **Skill Gap Analysis.** This process seeks to identify discrepancies between mentees' current abilities, knowledge, and behaviors and the desired capabilities through interviews, surveys, or focus groups. This data gathering could involve the target mentee population, their direct line manager, and, if circumstances permit, a selection of work colleagues. In addition, an evaluation of employee performance data can sometimes provide a 'bigger picture' of performance expectations.
4. **Making the Right Match**. Easier said than done! Here are a few suggestions that organizations could follow to make successful matches:
    a. *Define Clear Objectives of Mentorship Program.* All relevant stakeholders (mentors, mentees, line managers, and HR supporters) need to understand the purpose, process, timeline, and degree of commitment.

b. *Align Goals and Interests.* Take note of both the mentor's and mentee's goals, interests, and skills. When these elements align closely, mentoring relationships are much more likely to be fruitful and benefit all parties involved.
c. *Consider Compatibility.* Take note of both the mentor's and the mentee's personalities and communication styles when choosing a mentor/mentee pair. An introverted mentee may benefit from an outgoing mentor who can help them come out of their shell more readily.
d. *Training and support.* Mentors should receive proper training and assistance with building effective mentoring relationships. This could include guidance in areas like communication, feedback, and goal-setting – and reading this book!

Time frame

The duration of an in-house mentoring program depends on many variables. Mentoring programs typically last between several weeks and months or years. In practice, most formal mentoring programs last six months to one year[88]. Another study investigating the impact on organizational outcomes concluded that longer mentoring relationships (12+ months) were linked with greater levels of career success, job satisfaction, and reduced turnover intentions; although results depended on factors such as relationship quality and the amount of support

---

[88] Murray, M. 2017. "Mentoring for women: keys to success." *International Journal of Evidence-Based Coaching and Mentoring* 15, no. 2: 39-54.

received[89]. However, the optimal duration will vary depending on program goals, objectives, and other considerations. Here are a few factors to keep in mind when making this decision:

1. **Program goals.** It is essential for programs to align their duration with their stated objectives. If their intent is to develop specific skills or achieve specific outcomes, they must last for a certain period before ending.
2. **Mentor and mentee commitments**. The availability and commitment of mentors and mentees may affect the length of a program; if they can only commit for limited periods, programs must be structured.
3. **Program resources**: The resources at hand for any given program - funding, staff time, and technology – as well as competing with other organizational initiatives, can have an enormous impact on its duration.

Training mentors

Given the potential long-term value of mentoring in an organization, thought should be given to developing managers' competencies and confidence to act as effective mentors. Below are some key components that may make up such a development program:

---

[89] Keller, A. C., Bipp, T., Titz, S., & Schulte, S. 2021. "The effects of mentoring duration on career success, job satisfaction, and turnover intentions: The role of mentoring relationship quality and mentor support." *Journal of Vocational Behavior 129.*

☐ Structure and objectives of the mentoring program[90]

Topics would include a definition, benefits, and the type of relationship envisaged, including its duration and time commitment. Prospective mentors should also become familiar with their roles and responsibilities to their mentee and to the organization.

☐ Effective communication

As has been emphasized, communication skills matter enormously in mentoring. Topics might include active listening techniques, providing feedback, and giving constructive feedback.

☐ Goal setting and action planning

In this module, the focus should be on setting clear goals and objectives for mentoring relationships and on creating plans to achieve them. Managers should learn to help their mentees identify their strengths and weaknesses and develop plans to address them as needed.

☐ Coaching Skills

Although coaching is not the same as mentoring, some coaching skills can be usefully incorporated into a mentor's 'toolbox'. This would include asking powerful questions, offering support and encouragement, and keeping mentees accountable.

☐ Diversity

This module should address how to be an inclusive mentor and work effectively with employees from diverse

---

[90] Clutterbuck, D., & Megginson, D. 2020. *Techniques for coaching and mentoring* (3rd ed.). Routledge.

backgrounds. Managers should learn about unconscious bias and create safe mentoring environments that support growth.

☐ Legal and ethical issues

Mentoring relationships may raise legal and ethical concerns, including confidentiality, conflicts of interest, and boundaries, that need to be addressed in this module. A discussion of pathways to seek assistance in such circumstances should be part of the program content.

☐ Evaluation and feedback

Effective mentors must learn to assess the success of mentoring relationships and provide feedback to both mentees and organizations. What worked well? What didn't and why? By reflecting, recording, and communicating insights, feedback will be essential to the program's effectiveness.

Metrics for success

Despite the inherent challenges of evaluating mentoring's impact, it is equally important to pay sufficient attention to capturing its benefits. One recent study reviewed 112 other published studies on mentoring outcomes[91]. Their findings indicate that mentoring has moderate-to-large effects on job performance, career development, and retention, but only slight effects on psychological well-being. Based on this data, the authors conclude that the effectiveness of mentoring programs depends on a variety of factors, including the quality of

---

[91] Eby, L. T., Allen, T. D., Evans, S. C., Ng, T., & DuBois, D. L. 2021. "Does mentoring work? A meta-analytic review and research agenda." *Journal of Vocational Behavior 126.*

mentoring relationships, the level of organizational support, and the program's overall duration.

Return on investment of mentoring

Organizations can measure the effectiveness of their mentoring programs through various metrics:

- **Quantitative measures**. One way to gauge the Return on Investment (ROI) of mentoring programs is to measure changes in productivity, employee retention rates, and promotions/career advancements made available through mentor programs. Such measures enable organizations to gauge whether mentoring initiatives have had positive effects on employees.[92]
- **Qualitative measures**. Alongside quantitative metrics, qualitative metrics such as employee satisfaction and engagement levels must also be considered. Using surveys or focus groups, organizations can collect employee feedback regarding how the mentoring program impacts professional growth. A different approach to evaluating mentoring program effectiveness could also include:
- Whether initial goals and expectations were met.
- The degree to which the mentor and mentee were well-matched
- How well structured the mentoring program was, and whether there was sufficient support for the mentor as well as the mentee.

---

[92] Frink, D. D., & Anderson, M. 2021. "The Return on Investment of Executive Coaching and Mentoring." *Journal of Applied Leadership and Management* 9, no. 1: 72-89

- Whether the performance and commitment of the mentor and mentee were evaluated, and whether accountability for achieving broad outcomes was clear.[93]

Cost analysis. Another effective method for measuring mentoring returns is comparing its costs with its benefits. Organizations can calculate all training and development expenses related to mentoring programs, then compare these costs with the increased employee retention and productivity gains resulting from this investment.[94] Analyzing the costs associated with mentoring programs involves several steps, which include:

- **Locating direct costs.** Direct costs refer to expenses directly associated with running the mentoring program, such as materials, training costs, and staff time costs
- **Identification of indirect costs.** Indirect costs are expenses not directly associated with mentoring programs but incurred as a result of them; for instance, lost productivity or additional staff costs may arise. It is essential that these indirect costs be estimated and included in the total program costs when preparing budget projections.
- **Calculating benefits.** To assess the return on investment for mentoring programs, it's necessary to also calculate their benefits. Such benefits could include increased employee retention rates, greater productivity, and improved job satisfaction, all of which should be

---

[93] Chamorro-Premuzic, T. 2021. "Mentoring Programs Are a Waste of Money Unless They Have These Four Components." *Harvard Business Review*

[94] Liu, M., & McCarthy, A. M. 2022. "The Economic Value of Mentoring Programs for New Graduate Nurses: A Systematic Review." *Nursing Economics* 40, no. 1: 40-49.

quantified relative to total program expenses to determine the return on investment (ROI).

Benchmarking. The final piece is comparing the costs and benefits of benchmarking within your own organization with mentoring programs in similar Organizations. This sort of comparative data can be a useful tool for making informed decisions about effectiveness, cost-efficiency, and potential areas for improvement. This practice helps determine if it meets all its intended purposes while simultaneously pinpointing areas for development.

Benefits of mentoring

The Kirkpatrick model[95] is an established framework frequently used to evaluate education, training, and development initiatives. Using this approach, some pertinent measures of success can be identified to assess the mentoring program's value.

---

[95] https://kirkpatrickpartners.com/the-kirkpatrick-model/

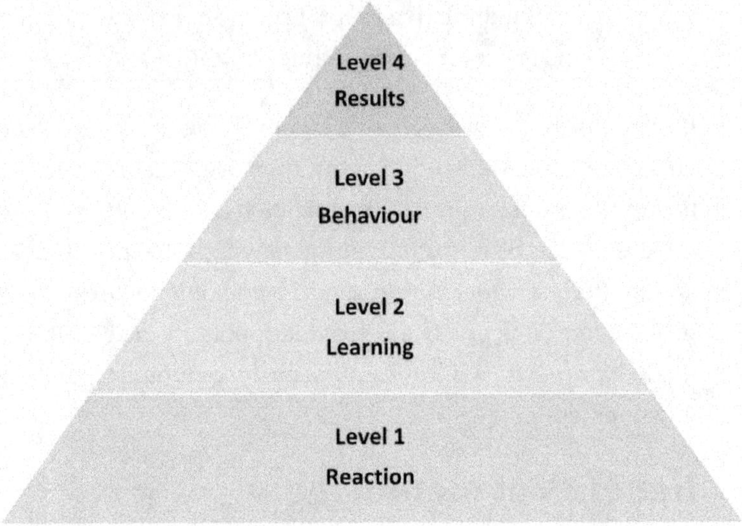

Level 4
Results

Level 3
Behaviour

Level 2
Learning

Level 1
Reaction

Level 1: Reaction[96]

In Level 1 measurements, the reactions of the mentee and mentor can be measured. For example, one way to get Level 1 feedback is to send out a survey to the mentor and mentees with questions such as:

- What was most meaningful in your participation in the mentoring program?
- On a scale of 1-5, how valuable has your mentoring experience been for your career?
- Did you enjoy participating in the program?

Sometimes referred to as a 'happy sheet', level 1 offers insight into participants' immediate responses. Relying solely on Level 1 feedback will usually not indicate the program's success.

---

[96] https://www.get.mentoringcomplete.com/blog/kirkpatrick-model-to-evaluate-your-mentoring-program

However, it is important to understand the experiences of both the mentee and the mentor in the program.

Level 2: Learning

Beyond participants' initial reactions, Level 2 feedback aims to measure how much people learn from the mentoring program. This is where metrics sometimes fail to catch all the learning taking place! The learning that goes on in a mentoring program isn't always technical or even skill-based. For example, in a mentoring program that seeks to increase diversity and inclusion company-wide, one objective might be to change mentors' (who are influential leaders in the organization) perceptions of individuals from diverse backgrounds. One way to measure this is through pre- and post-survey data on relevant perceptions and attitudes.

Level 3: Behavior

At this level, the model seeks to identify behavior change. Notoriously difficult to identify and track, behavior change could involve the acquisition of new technical or presentation skills, or indeed any other observable behavior. One approach to tracking this might be to ensure that both the mentor and the mentee know what is expected. Behavior changes are very important to mentoring programs that focus on leadership development or other skill development. Ideally, mentees will begin making behavioral changes throughout the program. If they are not, it might be important to investigate why new learning isn't being applied.

For example, a mentee might be learning new leadership skills through the mentoring program, but these new skills are unlikely to be applied if the mentee's manager doesn't support the leadership perspective presented in the program.

Some ways to measure behavioral changes include interviews and observations. It is a good idea to get others involved in providing information. For example, the mentee's direct reports might be able to provide behavioral observations that would help measure the success of the mentoring program. Alternatively, providing pre- and post-mentoring 360-degree evaluations from the mentee's peers, focusing on their observations, is often helpful.

Level 4: Impact

At this level, the focus is to determine whether the organization/mentoring sponsor can perceive any improvement in the objectives the program was intended to achieve. The challenge is to determine whether there is causality between the mentoring and the results captured, or whether other factors may have interfered (positively or negatively) to 'muddy the waters'. As you can imagine, given the complexity and multiple factors that can affect mentoring outcomes, this is hard to assess.

Some measures are:

- ☐ Increased employee retention comparing individuals mentored versus those who have not been mentored
- ☐ Increased productivity and/or job performance
- ☐ Higher morale and engagement scores (based on employee attitude surveys)

In many organizations, there is an ethos of ensuring that all investments deliver an acceptable ROI. Overall, training and development is tricky and often extremely convoluted. Mentoring can be even more difficult. There are (at least) two reasons why this is problematic.

The first is the timeframe. Mentoring takes place over a long period (usually more than 6 months), and its impact needs to be measured over the years. As any good financial analyst will tell you, making a proper assessment requires weighing future benefits against present expenditure.

The second challenge is the cost of maintaining a mentoring program. Usually, the external costs are relatively limited (compared to a formal training and development program). However, there are some hidden costs, including the time mentors spend meeting with mentees and reflecting on and organizing development opportunities. A similar time investment can be recognized by the mentees as well, as they will have to divert some of their efforts away from job-related deliverables to satisfy the requirements agreed with their mentor.

Debrief

Here's the uncomfortable reality about mentoring ROI: the benefits manifest over years; unfortunately, the costs appear immediately. This mismatch explains why finance directors question the value of mentoring programs even when research consistently shows moderate to large effects on job performance, career development, and retention. The challenge isn't proving mentoring works; it's measuring impact across timeframes that exceed most strategic planning horizons.

The Kirkpatrick model's four levels address this systematically. Level 1 (reaction) provides immediate feedback but proves little: "happy sheets" measure satisfaction, not impact. Level 2 (learning) captures knowledge acquisition but not application. Level 3 (behavior change) shows actual skill development, though it requires sustained observation. Level 4 (organizational impact) demonstrates real value but struggles with causality: did mentoring improve retention, or were other factors involved?

The seven mentor training components are not bureaucratic box-ticking. Without training in program structure, communication skills, goal-setting, coaching techniques, diversity awareness, ethical issues, and evaluation methods, you're essentially asking well-meaning amateurs to wing it. Some will succeed through natural ability; most won't. Training transforms good intentions into genuine capability.

Your next step: If you're designing a program, resist pressure to show immediate ROI. Instead, commit to a 12-month minimum duration, implement all four Kirkpatrick levels from the outset, and prepare stakeholders for long-term measurement. If you're evaluating an existing program, audit against the seven training components. Missing ones explain most program failures. Add them before declaring the program unsuccessful.

12. Getting started

Turning polite enthusiasm into an actual meeting

TL;DR

Theory is done; now comes the awkward bit: starting. This chapter strips away the mystique with a practical walkthrough of what happens before, during, and after that first meeting. Begin by genuinely getting to know each other; vulnerability builds trust faster than credentials. Focus the first meeting on the mentee's story rather than yours, and resist the urge to solve problems before you have understood them. Set broad direction collaboratively, then hand the details to the Mentoring Action Plan in Chapter 13.

The gap between intending and doing

Most mentoring relationships that fail never get started. The intention is there: two people agree that mentoring would be valuable, exchange pleasantries about finding a time to meet, and then allow competing priorities to quietly bury the idea. Research on formal mentoring programs consistently finds that between a third and a half of pairings end before the initial time commitment is met (Heppe, Kupersmidt, and Kef, 2024), and many of those never progress beyond the agreement to meet. The relationship does not collapse; it simply never launches.[97]

The reasons are predictable. Both parties are busy. Neither is entirely sure who should send the first calendar invite. The mentor does not want to come across as pushy; the mentee does not want to come across as demanding. A week passes, then a month, and the window of enthusiasm closes. What began as a genuine offer has stalled into an increasingly awkward obligation that neither party wants to acknowledge.

This chapter exists to close that gap. The advice here is deliberately practical and unglamorous: it covers the logistics, the preparation, and the small disciplines that turn a good intention into a functioning partnership. None of it is intellectually difficult. All of it requires someone to go first. That someone, in most cases, should be you.

---

[97] Heppe, Eline C. M., Janis B. Kupersmidt, and Sabina Kef. "Reasons for Premature Closure of a Mentoring Relationship: A Qualitative Study of Mentoring Youth With a Visual Impairment." *Journal of Adolescent Research* 39, no. 3 (2024): 711–45. https://doi.org/10.1177/07435584211034874.

Getting to know each other

If you do not know the prospective mentee well, ask them to send you a brief, up-to-date CV or professional summary before your first meeting. Send one of your own in return. This exchange achieves two things: it gives both parties material to prepare with, and it establishes a tone of reciprocity from the outset. Mentoring relationships that begin with information flowing in only one direction, the mentor asks, the mentee answers, tend to replicate the power dynamics of a performance review rather than a developmental conversation.

Look for common ground but be honest about differences too. Shared experiences (a similar career path, a common employer, overlapping technical expertise) can accelerate rapport, but surface-level similarity is not the same as a genuine connection. Pedersen et al. (2022) found that perceived 'deep-level' similarity, shared attitudes, values, and perspectives, predicted mentoring relationship quality far more strongly than demographic similarity, such as gender or ethnicity.[98] A mentor and mentee who attended the same university but hold fundamentally different views about leadership will find that common ground is thinner than expected. What matters is whether the two of you see the world in broadly compatible ways, not whether your CVs look alike.

One step that many mentors skip, and should not, is thinking about what they hope to gain from the relationship and being willing to say so. *"I'm looking forward to this because I want to*

---

[98] Pedersen, Rachelle M., C. F. Ferguson, M. Estrada, P. W. Schultz, A. Woodcock, and P. R. Hernandez. "Similarity and Contact Frequency Promote Mentorship Quality Among Hispanic Undergraduates in STEM." *CBE - Life Sciences Education* 21, no. 2 (2022): ar27. https://doi.org/10.1187/cbe.21-10-0305.

understand how the graduate intake sees the business, " or "*I find that mentoring keeps me honest about my own development,* " are not admissions of self-interest. They signal that this is a two-way relationship and give the mentee permission to be equally direct about their own expectations. Sarabipour et al. (2022) emphasize that successful mentoring relationships are mentee-driven but mentor-guided, with both sides willing to invest time and energy, and that reciprocity of purpose is a distinguishing feature of relationships that endure.[99] Vulnerability builds trust faster than credentials do.

The first meeting

First meetings are rarely comfortable, and pretending otherwise does no one any good. The mentor wonders whether they have anything useful to offer; the mentee wonders whether the mentor will take them seriously. Both parties are performing slightly edited versions of themselves. This is normal. It passes.

The single most useful thing a mentor can do in the first meeting is listen more than they talk. The temptation, particularly for experienced managers who are accustomed to being the most senior person in the room, is to establish credibility by sharing their own story, offering early advice, or demonstrating expertise. **Resist this**! The first meeting is about the mentee's story, not yours. Ask about their career so far, what brought them to this point, what they are finding challenging, and what they

---

[99] Sarabipour, Sarvenaz, Sarah J. Hainer, Feyza Nur Arslan, Charlotte M. de Winde, Emily Furlong, Natalia Bielczyk, Nafisa M. Jadavji, Aparna P. Shah, and Sejal Davla. "Building and Sustaining Mentor Interactions as a Mentee." *The FEBS Journal* 289, no. 6 (2022): 1374–84. https://doi.org/10.1111/febs.15823.

hope the mentoring relationship might help with. Your job in this meeting is to understand, not to solve.

Feng, Nakkula, and Jiang (2024) found that mentors who combined relational purposes, building connection, showing genuine interest, with developmental ones produced significantly higher relationship quality than those who focused immediately on skills, goals, or career planning.[100] In other words, the early meetings are where the relational foundation gets built, and mentors who jump to advice-giving before that foundation is in place often find their guidance politely received but rarely acted upon. The mentee has not yet decided whether this person's opinion is worth taking seriously. That decision is made during exactly these early conversations.

A practical structure for the first meeting: spend the first half exploring the mentee's background, aspirations, and current challenges. Spend the second half discussing how the relationship might work: frequency, format, mutual expectations, and what each party will bring. If you asked the mentee to complete the Career Vision template from Chapter 4, this is the natural moment to discuss it. Close by agreeing on a specific date for the next meeting before you leave the room. If that date is not in the diary before you stand up, the probability of it happening drops sharply.

Scheduling and logistics

How you treat the diary signals how seriously you take the relationship. A mentor who repeatedly reschedules, consistently

---

[100] Feng, Yihe, Michael Nakkula, and Yuyang Jiang. "Toward Building a Better Scaffold: How Types of Mentor Support Inform Mentor-Mentee Match Relationship Quality." *Frontiers in Psychology* 14 (2024): 1259040. https://doi.org/10.3389/fpsyg.2023.1259040.

arrives late, or squeezes mentoring into the fifteen minutes between other commitments is communicating something the mentee will notice long before either party acknowledges it aloud.

Aim for sessions of around 60 minutes. Shorter meetings tend to produce rushed conversations that stay on the surface; significantly longer ones can exhaust both parties and make scheduling harder. Some pairs find that 45 minutes works well once the relationship is established and the conversations have a clear focus. Others prefer 90 minutes at wider intervals. The right cadence is whatever both parties can sustain consistently; regularity matters more than duration.

The critical threshold appears to be around twice a year: drop below it, and you are essentially starting from scratch each time, unable to build on previous conversations or track meaningful progress. Monthly or bimonthly meetings work well for most pairs, providing enough frequency to maintain momentum without creating an onerous commitment.

Location matters more than most mentors assume. A meeting room with a glass wall facing the open-plan office is not the same as a private space where the mentee feels safe discussing genuine concerns. Meeting away from the workplace, over coffee, or during a walk, can sometimes produce more honest conversations than any meeting room. Virtual meetings are a practical necessity for many pairs and can work well, though they require more deliberate effort to build rapport (Chapter 17 explores the specific challenges of virtual and hybrid mentoring in detail).

Setting direction

Once the first meeting has established a working rapport, the question of direction needs attention. What does the mentee want to achieve? What can the mentor realistically offer? These questions deserve honest answers rather than aspirational ones.

The goal at this stage is broad alignment, not a detailed plan. You are trying to establish a shared sense of what this relationship is for: whether that is building confidence in senior-level interactions, preparing for a career transition, developing a specific skill set, or simply having access to an experienced sounding board. Precision comes later. Chapter 13 introduces the Mentoring Action Plan framework, which provides a structured tool for translating these initial conversations into documented goals, development activities, and review points. There is no need to duplicate that work here; what matters now is that both parties leave the early meetings with a clear enough sense of direction that the relationship has purpose.

Two points are worth emphasizing. First, the mentee's goals will change. What seems urgent in month one often looks quite different by month six. Treat early goals as a working hypothesis rather than a binding contract, and revisit them regularly. Second, direction-setting should include something for the mentor. Asking yourself, "What am I hoping to learn from this?" at the outset is not self-interested: it is honest, and it reinforces the principle that this is a mutual relationship.

Building early habits

The first three meetings establish the habits that will define the relationship. If you ask the mentee to prepare topics in advance of the first meeting and they do, that expectation becomes the norm. If you let the first three meetings happen without any preparation from either side, the relationship has already settled into a pattern of casual drift that is surprisingly difficult to correct.

A few habits are worth establishing from the start. Ask the mentee to send a brief note before each meeting with a few bullet points on what they would like to discuss. This gives you time to reflect and prepare, and it signals that the meeting has an agenda rather than being an open-ended chat. At the end of each meeting, agree on specific actions for both parties and confirm the date and time of the next session. These small disciplines prevent the gradual loosening of commitment that Chapter 14 describes as "momentum killers."

Seeking feedback early is equally important. At the end of the second or third meeting, ask the mentee directly: *"How is this working for you? Is there anything you'd like me to do differently?"* The question needs to be genuine, not a perfunctory closing remark delivered while gathering up papers. Most mentees will not volunteer criticism of their mentor unprompted, particularly early in the relationship when the power dynamic is still unresolved. Thurman (2024) notes that when roles, expectations, and goals are not clearly defined from the outset, frustration builds on both sides, and that regular, honest communication is the single most effective preventative measure.[101] Asking explicitly and responding well to whatever they say teaches the mentee that honest feedback is welcome.

Share your own reflections, too. *"I felt that session was more useful when we focused on the specific situation rather than talking in*

---

[101] Thurman, Sabrina. "*Help!: When Problems Arise in Mentoring Relationships*." Center for Engaged Learning, Elon University. November 8, 2024. https://www.centerforengagedlearning.org/help-when-problems-arise-in-mentoring-relationships/.

general terms. Did you feel the same?" This kind of modeling normalizes reflective practice and helps both parties calibrate what "good" looks like for this relationship.

When to talk about endings

It may seem premature to discuss endings when the relationship has barely started. It isn't. Acknowledging early on that this relationship will eventually reach a natural conclusion, whether in six months or three years, removes the awkwardness of bringing it up later. A brief conversation in the first or second meeting about what success might look like and how you will both know when the relationship has served its purpose gives the partnership direction and a reference point for future review.

Chapter 16 covers the transition process in detail, including how to recognize the signals, conduct a closing review, and manage the shift from a structured mentoring relationship to whatever comes next. The point here is simply this: begin with the end in mind. Relationships that start with an honest conversation about their anticipated scope are far easier to conclude well than those that drift along until mutual awkwardness forces a quiet withdrawal.

Exercise: The first meeting planner

This exercise helps you prepare for your first mentoring meeting. Complete it before the session and bring it with you: not to follow rigidly, but to ensure you have thought through the key elements.

Part 1: Before the meeting

Write brief answers to the following:

- What do I know about this person already? (CV, reputation, mutual contacts, prior conversations.)
- What common ground might we share? (Background, interests, career experiences, sector knowledge.)
- What do I hope to gain from this mentoring relationship? (Be honest, and be prepared to share this.)
- What is one thing I could share about myself that would signal openness and build trust?

Part 2: During the meeting

Use these prompts to guide the conversation. You do not need to cover all of them: let the discussion flow naturally, but make sure the essentials (marked with *) are addressed:

- *Ask the mentee about their career story so far. Listen for themes, turning points, and what energizes them.
- *Ask what they hope to get from the mentoring relationship. (If they completed a Career Vision template, use it as a starting point.)
- Share what drew you to mentoring and what you hope to learn from the relationship.
- Discuss practical logistics: preferred frequency, meeting length, location, and how you will communicate between sessions.
- Agree on the date, time, and location of the next meeting before you leave the room.

Part 3: After the meeting

Within 24 hours, note your reflections:

- What struck me most about the conversation?
- What does this person seem to need most? Is that something I can help with?
- What will I do differently in the next meeting?

- Have I sent a brief follow-up message confirming what we agreed?

Debrief

The gap between "we should mentor" and "we are mentoring" is where most potential relationships go to die. Research consistently finds that between a third and a half of formally arranged mentoring pairings end before the initial time commitment is met: not always because the match was wrong, but often because neither party took responsibility for turning intention into action. This chapter addresses that gap with unglamorous but essential practicalities: preparation, first meetings, scheduling, direction-setting, and early habits.

The reciprocity matters. Mentors who send their own CVs, articulate their own learning goals, and seek feedback on their own performance are not diluting their authority; they are modeling exactly the openness they want from their mentee. Relationships that begin with information flowing in one direction tend to stay that way. Those who establish mutual exchange early build the kind of trust that makes later, more challenging conversations possible.

The scheduling guidance deserves emphasis: 60-minute sessions, a distraction-free environment, and a regular cadence. These are not suggestions for the particularly organized; they are minimum standards for showing respect. Keeping your email open during a mentoring conversation signals that anything more urgent than your mentee's development will interrupt them. It will.

Your next step: If you have been meaning to start mentoring someone, stop reading and send the calendar invite now: this week, not "when things calm down." If you are already mentoring, review the early habits section. Are you asking for topics in advance? Seeking feedback after meetings? Confirming next steps before you leave the room? If not, add these to your next session. Small disciplines prevent large drift.

13. Mentoring action plan

How to stop having the same conversation every three months

TL;DR:

Vague good intentions do not survive contact with busy schedules, which is why this chapter introduces the Mentoring Action Plan: a framework that transforms aspirations into structured developmental partnerships. But here is the critical point: this is not a rigid contract. Visions evolve, goals shift, activities must adapt. The plan's value lies in maintaining alignment between aspiration and action. Regular reviews prevent drift and keep it relevant, rather than letting it become another document gathering digital dust.

Scaffolding, not a script

Without a written plan, mentoring relationships can drift. Research conducted on behalf of the Association for Talent Development found that mentoring programs with documented action plans achieved 43% higher goal attainment rates than those relying solely on informal conversations.[102]

The difference isn't subtle: mentees working from action plans reported clearer expectations, better progress tracking, and significantly less frustration about whether their mentoring relationship was "working." Yet despite this evidence, many mentors resist creating formal plans, worried that they will impose unnecessary bureaucracy or stifle the spontaneity of good mentoring conversations. This chapter addresses that concern head-on: a well-designed action plan amplifies rather than constrains the adaptive, responsive mentoring this book advocates for.

The key to effective action planning lies in co-creation. Work undertaken by Allen and Eby (2007) demonstrates that mentees who actively participate in designing their development plans show 38% higher commitment levels and greater follow-through on agreed actions than those presented with mentor-designed plans[103]. Think of the action plan as scaffolding rather than a script: it provides structure that both parties can reference when conversations meander, whilst leaving ample room for the improvisation that responsive mentoring requires. When you and your mentee build the plan together, you are establishing shared ownership of the relationship's direction rather than imposing your agenda.

The three-component framework presented here, personal vision, goals and objectives, and development activities, creates

---

[102] Association for Talent Development. 2017. The value of evaluation: Making training evaluations more effective. Alexandria, VA: ATD Press.

[103] Allen, T. D., and L. T. Eby, eds. 2007. *The Blackwell handbook of mentoring: A multiple perspectives approach*. Malden, MA: Blackwell Publishing

alignment without rigidity. Research from Kram and Isabella (1985) shows that mentees who can articulate how their immediate development activities connect to longer-term aspirations demonstrate significantly higher resilience when setbacks occur.[104] The action plan becomes the reference point for those "*how does this fit with where I'm heading?*" conversations that distinguish developmental mentoring from casual advice-giving. More, having the plan documented means neither of you will waste time in your next session trying to remember what you agreed to three months ago.

Mentoring action plan framework

The framework shown here deliberately moves from broad to specific, mirroring how career development unfolds in practice. Your mentee starts by articulating their personal vision, where they see themselves in roughly five years, which provides the "north star" that makes all subsequent decisions easier. From this vision flows four specific goals and objectives that translate aspiration into actionable targets. Finally, each goal breaks down into concrete development activities. This comprises the actual work your mentee will do. This cascading structure prevents the common trap where mentees enthusiastically collect development experiences that do not advance their careers. When your mentee can trace each activity back to a goal and, ultimately, to their overarching vision, they're building a career rather than just accumulating credentials.

Notice what the framework doesn't include: rigid timelines, mandatory monthly reviews, or complicated progress metrics.

---

[104] Kram, K. E., & Isabella, L. A. 1985. "Mentoring alternatives: The role of peer relationships in career development." *Academy of Management Journal* 28, no. 1: 110-132.

That is intentional. The power of this tool lies in its simplicity: it fits on a single page, takes perhaps an hour to complete initially, and requires only brief quarterly reviews to stay current. Some mentors laminate their mentees' completed plans and reference them at the start of each session; others photograph them and revisit them whenever conversations drift into unproductive territory. The format matters less than the practice of regularly checking alignment. Your mentee's vision will evolve as they gain experience and exposure, their goals will shift as some prove more achievable than others, and development activities will be added, completed, or abandoned based on what becomes available. The framework accommodates all of this: it's a working document, not a contract.

Exercise: Mentoring action plan

Personal vision: (~5 years)	Goals & objectives		
	1.		
	2.		
	3.		
	4.		
	Goal 1:	Development Activity 1:	
		Development Activity 2:	
		Development Activity 3:	
	Goal 2:	Development Activity 1:	
		Development Activity 2:	
		Development Activity 3:	
	Goal 3:	Development Activity 1:	
		Development Activity 2:	
		Development Activity 3:	

Personal vision

Formulating a vision statement is the ability to see yourself in a situation that has not yet occurred. The following questions will help you focus on creating a vision of where you see yourself in five years.

Some useful questions to start a dialogue on this topic are:

- ☐ Where do you want to be?
- ☐ What do you want to be known for?
- ☐ What do you stand for?
- ☐ Why do you want to achieve this?

There is no requirement for a personal vision to remain static! Circumstances and personal interests change, so it can be viewed with some fluidity. Even so, it is helpful to have a starting point based on current perceptions and interests.

The "why" question matters more than most mentors realize. Research by Deci and Ryan (2000) on self-determination shows that individuals pursuing goals driven by intrinsic motivation, personal values, genuine interest, and internal satisfaction experience significantly greater persistence and well-being than those pursuing externally imposed targets.[105] When your mentee can articulate *why* they want to become a finance director or move into operations, you're helping them distinguish between goals they genuinely own versus those they think they *should* want because of family expectations, peer pressure, or assumptions about what success looks like. A mentee who wants

---

[105] Deci, E. L., & Ryan, R. M. 2000. The "what" and "why" of goal pursuits: Human needs and the self-determination of behavior. *Psychological Inquiry* 11, no. 4: 227-268

the corner office because they value strategic influence will make different choices and weather setbacks differently than one who wants it because their colleagues are climbing the organizational ladder and they feel left behind. The vision conversation isn't complete until you've helped your mentee connect their aspirations to their deeper motivations. Without this, you're building on sand.

Goals & objectives

After a vision statement is formulated, the next step is to create solid goals and objectives. These goals and objectives will be the driving force of your mentoring relationship and provide a starting point for you and your mentor to develop learning activities.

The mentee can initiate, refine, and clarify goals and objectives, but these are often developed with the mentor during the first few mentoring meetings. Identifying relevant goals and objectives is an important component of the mentor/mentee relationship. It should be revisited regularly to check for additions, deletions, and changes throughout the relationship.

The goals your mentee sets will make or break their action plan, yet this is where most mentoring relationships stumble. Research shows that specific, challenging goals lead to higher performance than vague "do your best" aspirations, but there is a catch.[106] Goals imposed by others trigger compliance at best and resistance at worst, whilst self-generated goals activate genuine commitment. Your job as a mentor isn't to write your mentee's goals for them; it is to help them articulate goals that

---

[106] Locke, E. A., & Latham, G. P. 2002. "Building a practically useful theory of goal setting and task motivation: A 35-year odyssey." *American Psychologist* 57, no. 9: 705-717.

are specific enough to guide action yet flexible enough to accommodate the surprises every career encounters. The examples below span three domains that effective goals typically address: building expertise, expanding relationships, and understanding how your organization works.

Skills and expertise development:

- ☐ Develop advanced data visualization skills to present quarterly results more compellingly.
- ☐ Build confidence, facilitating difficult team conversations without escalating to my manager
- ☐ Master the new CRM system well enough to train others in my department
- ☐ Learn enough about our supply chain to identify improvement opportunities in my area

Relationship and network building:

- ☐ Establish working relationships with peers in marketing and operations to better understand cross-functional dependencies.
- ☐ Build credibility with the senior leadership team through contributing valuable insights in monthly reviews
- ☐ Develop a mentoring relationship with someone in finance to demystify budget processes
- ☐ Create stronger connections with our European colleagues to understand regional market differences

Organizational navigation:

- ☐ Understand how funding decisions get made beyond the formal approval process
- ☐ Identify who the real influencers are in driving our digital transformation agenda
- ☐ Learn which committees matter versus which exist for show
- ☐ Map the informal networks that get things done when formal channels stall

Notice what these goals share: they're specific enough that you and your mentee will know whether they've been achieved, yet broad enough to allow multiple paths to success. "Build my reputation as an engineer" sounds laudable but offers no guidance about what to do differently tomorrow. "Build credibility with the senior leadership team through contributing valuable insights in monthly reviews" points toward observable actions your mentee can practice. When your mentee brings vague goals to the table, your first step is to help them sharpen the focus until the goal suggests its own development activities. That's when you know you're onto something useful.

SMART objective setting

When supporting a mentee in clarifying goals and objectives, a mentor can use familiar tools and techniques. For example, a SMART objective-setting framework may be useful, as shown below.

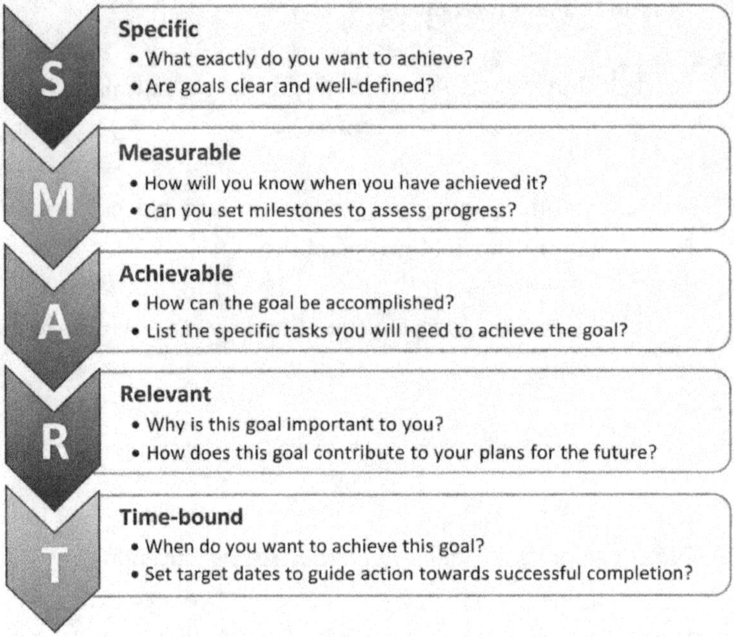

S **Specific**
- What exactly do you want to achieve?
- Are goals clear and well-defined?

M **Measurable**
- How will you know when you have achieved it?
- Can you set milestones to assess progress?

A **Achievable**
- How can the goal be accomplished?
- List the specific tasks you will need to achieve the goal?

R **Relevant**
- Why is this goal important to you?
- How does this goal contribute to your plans for the future?

T **Time-bound**
- When do you want to achieve this goal?
- Set target dates to guide action towards successful completion?

Development activities

Development activities are the actions undertaken by both the mentor and the mentee to fulfill the mentee's agreed goals & objectives. They are the practical "stepping-stones" between where a mentee is now and where they might wish to be in the future. By identifying the developmental areas with the greatest growth potential (which should already have been defined in the mentoring goals and objectives), the mentee will experience greater rewards at the end of the program and beyond!

Help the mentee identify short- and long-term activities you can support. These may emerge at any point in the relationship. Often, mentors find this part of the process the most challenging and rewarding, as it may require drawing on their own insights, contacts, and experience.

To develop activities, refer back to the established mentoring goals and objectives. Most successful plans are those that have a range of learning activities that encourage:

- ✓ Developmental project. (E.g., special project, making a presentation, etc.)
- ✓ Networking opportunity. (E.g., shadowing, situational mentoring, etc.)
- ✓ Learning from challenging experiences or "stretch assignments." (E.g., project outside of department, leadership role, etc.)

A discussion that a mentor might have with a mentee is which development activities to prioritize. A framework for this could be the Success Triangle (shown below).[107] Think about what side of the Success Triangle the mentee would like to work on. Brainstorm some possible activities with your mentee to help them reach their goal.

---

[107] Drahosz, K. W., & Rhodes, D. C. 1997. The Success Triangle. *Dynamic Mentoring* training materials. The Training Connection

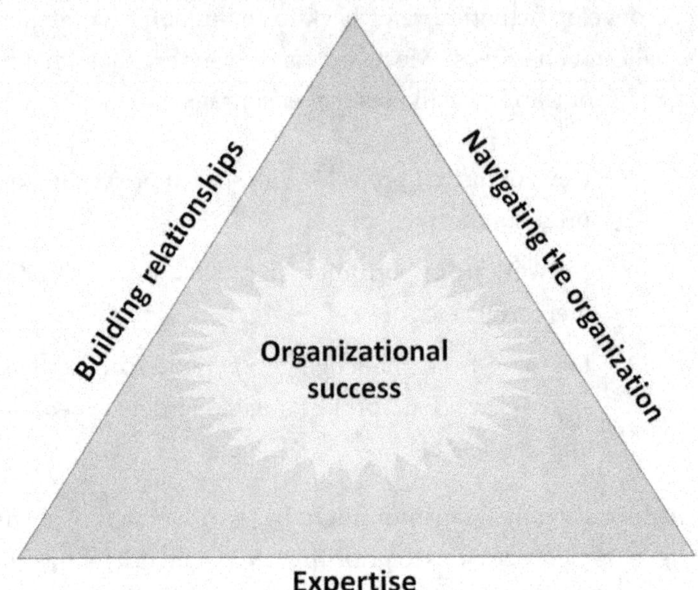

Expertise - how effective an individual is at mastering the expertise required of their job or career field. As a mentor, can you help the mentee clarify which areas of expertise they want to strengthen? Can you help them build their expertise – or at least set them up on the right track?

Building relationships - how effective an individual is at building relationships and connections with others. As a mentor, you are not expected to be the source of all knowledge! Can you provide introductions or opportunities for the mentee to build their own network of people they should know? Inviting a mentee to sit in on a meeting, conference, or presentation is a useful first step.

Navigating the organization - how effectively someone is at understanding and navigating the organization and its formal and informal structures. Most mentors know there are formal organizational structures and hierarchies, as well as informal relationships that span across internal units or departments.

Being effective in any organization requires skillful awareness of both! For mentees, organizational structures and what people do in different parts of the organization may be a complete mystery. Therefore, finding a way to allow mentees to learn more about other parts of the organization – as well as the people who fulfill the different roles - can be extremely useful.

Alignment

An important role a mentor can fulfill is to regularly review the alignment among the Personal Vision, Goals & Objectives, and Development activities. Over time, the mentee's personal vision might change. For example, as their awareness of new opportunities within the organization becomes apparent, their career plans may shift. Therefore, occasionally referring back to the Personal Vision statement and checking how it might evolve may be helpful.

Similarly, the goals & objectives component of the Mentor Action Plan should also be re-examined. Some goals may be more easily achieved than others. As a mentor, you might want to discuss your mentee's progress toward their goals and where additional support might be helpful.

Below are a few lessons I have learned (*and remembered!*):

- ☐ **Do the Goals & Objectives still fit with the Personal Vision?** What changes might be helpful in the light of new experience?
- ☐ What additional Goals & Objectives have emerged that might help the mentee fulfill their vision?
- ☐ **CAUTION**: **Avoid 'mission creep'** – a situation which can occur when an excessive number of goals & objectives can overlap and become counterproductive. As with

organizational goals, the fewer and simpler the goals, the more likely they are to be understood and acted upon.

Debrief

Let's return to that 43% statistic: mentoring programs with documented action plans achieve nearly half again as many goals as those relying on informal conversations. That's not a rounding error; it's the difference between mentoring that genuinely develops people and mentoring that feels supportive but delivers little. Yet most mentors resist creating plans, worried about bureaucracy. The framework in this chapter directly addresses that concern: one-page, quarterly reviews, and enough flexibility to accommodate the reality that careers rarely unfold as planned.

The co-creation principle matters enormously. When Allen and Eby (2007) found that mentees who design their own plans show 38% higher commitment, they weren't discovering rocket science; they were confirming what you already know from experience. People support what they create. The mentor who presents a completed action plan to their mentee has unwittingly transformed a developmental partnership into a compliance exercise. Your job isn't to write your mentee's plan; it's to ask the questions that help them write it themselves.

The three-component cascade, vision flows to goals, goals flow to activities, prevents the credential-collecting trap, in which mentees accumulate experiences that don't advance their careers. The Success Triangle offers a diagnostic when mentees struggle to prioritize: Are they weak on expertise, relationships, or organizational navigation? Each domain requires different development activities, and trying to strengthen all three simultaneously guarantees mediocre progress across the board.

Better to make substantial progress on one side of the triangle than marginal gains on all three.

The alignment conversation matters most. Personal visions evolve, goals shift, and development activities must adapt. The mentors who succeed with action plans aren't those who enforce rigid adherence to what was agreed six months ago; they're those who regularly check whether the plan still serves the mentee's current needs. That quarterly review prevents both drift (where conversations meander without purpose) and mission creep (where enthusiasm generates an unmanageable list of objectives). Simple question for each review: "Given what you've learned in the past three months, does this plan still point you toward where you want to go?"

Your next step: If you're starting a new mentoring relationship, schedule time in your first three meetings to build the action plan together. Don't rush it; the hour invested in co-creating a solid plan saves countless hours of meandering conversations later. If you are already mentoring without a documented plan, propose creating one retrospectively based on what you've already discussed. Your mentee will likely feel relief rather than resistance, and finally, clarity about what you're trying to achieve together.

14. Maintaining momentum

How to avoid the 'We Should Really Catch Up Sometime' Death Spiral

TL;DR:

> Mentoring relationships are far easier to maintain than to restart, yet most mentors do not realize momentum has stalled until it is too late. This chapter covers the predictable momentum killers (competing priorities, unclear next steps, invisible progress, purpose misalignment, and mentor over-functioning). The underlying message: gaps beyond eight to ten weeks effectively reset a mentoring relationship, forcing you to rebuild trust before meaningful work can resume. Prevention beats recovery every time.

The relationship between a mentor and a mentee is typically expected to last a long time, with a range of interactions, including face-to-face sessions, telephone calls, messages, and other methods as required. In organizations that initiate a formal mentoring program, the duration is usually at least 6 months, but often lasts much longer!

The paradox of momentum

Think of mentoring momentum like riding a bicycle uphill while carrying groceries: once you're moving, it's surprisingly manageable, but stop pedaling, and suddenly you're wrestling gravity, a wobbly frame, and a rogue bag of oranges threatening to escape. Newton's first law applies beautifully here: mentoring relationships in motion tend to stay in motion (conversations build naturally, trust deepens, progress compounds), while mentoring relationships at rest tend to stay at rest (every interaction requires Herculean effort just to remember where you left off). The cruel physics of the situation is that maintaining momentum takes perhaps 20% of the energy required to restart it, yet we consistently fool ourselves into thinking "we'll just pick up again next month" after a gap. We won't. We'll spend the first 30 minutes of that meeting reestablishing rapport, the next 20 apologizing for the delay, and the final 10 minutes mentoring, assuming the meeting happens at all and doesn't get bumped by the seventeen things that now feel more urgent, precisely because the mentoring relationship has lost its forward momentum. The lesson? Keep pedaling. The oranges are depending on you.

Like many human relationships, mentoring relationships are far easier to maintain than to restart. Experience shows that once momentum stalls, you're not simply picking up where you left off: you're essentially beginning again, rebuilding trust, re-establishing patterns, and reconstructing the psychological safety that took months to develop. Understanding why consistent engagement matters isn't about adding more to your already overflowing calendar; it's about preventing the far more time-consuming task of relationship repair.

Compound effect of maintaining consistency

Research on habit formation reveals a counterintuitive finding: consistency matters more than frequency. Psychologists Lally and Gardner's work on automaticity demonstrates that behaviors become "second nature" through repetition in consistent contexts, not through intensive bursts of activity. [108] Their research tracked participants' formation of new habits over 12 weeks and found that automaticity, the point at which behavior becomes effortless, developed through repeated actions in stable contexts. Missing a single opportunity didn't derail the process, but inconsistent performance significantly hindered progress.[109]

The same principle applies to mentoring relationships. Meeting monthly for six months builds more relationship capital than three intensive sessions followed by a four-month gap. Why? Because each interaction reinforces the pattern, deepens understanding, and builds on previous conversations. Your mentee begins to anticipate your meetings, mentally preparing questions and reflections between sessions. When gaps extend beyond 8-10 weeks, this anticipatory engagement evaporates: the

---

[108] Lally, P., & Gardner, B. 2013. "Promoting habit formation." *Health Psychology Review* 7, no. sup1: S137-S158

[109] Lally, P., van Jaarsveld, C.H., Potts, H.W., & Wardle, J. 2010. "How are habits formed: Modeling habit formation in the real world." *European Journal of Social Psychology* 40, no. 6: 998-1009

relationship hasn't ended, but its momentum has, and you're effectively starting fresh each time.

The frequency of contact also correlates with relationship quality in ways that matter for actual outcomes. Research from the National Academies of Sciences found that communication frequency, along with shared experiences and perceived emotional quality, is positively associated with mentees' self-efficacy, academic success, and professional identity development.[110] This isn't about logging more hours; it's about maintaining the thread of continuity that allows deeper work to emerge.

Momentum killers

Several predictable culprits derail even well-intentioned mentoring relationships:

- ☐ **Competing priorities without renegotiation**. Everyone is busy, that's not the issue. The problem arises when increased demands on either party aren't addressed through explicit discussion of adjusting the meeting frequency or format. The relationship drifts not because people don't care, but because nobody names the drift.
- ☐ **Lack of clear next steps**. Meetings that end without concrete commitments, even small ones, signal that the relationship lacks direction. If your mentee can't answer "What am I working on before we next meet?"

---

[110] National Academies of Sciences, Engineering, and Medicine. 2019. *The Science of Effective Mentorship in STEMM*. Washington, DC: The National Academies Press.

immediately after your conversation, momentum has already begun slipping.

- ☐ **Absence of visible progress**. When weeks pass without tangible progress toward goals, both parties begin to question the relationship's value. Progress doesn't require dramatic breakthroughs, but it does require change, however incremental.
- ☐ **Misalignment around purpose**. If you believe the mentoring relationship aims toward career strategy while your mentee seeks technical skill development, every interaction will feel slightly off-target to someone. Unaddressed, these misalignments compound into disengagement.
- ☐ **Over-reliance on the mentor to drive contact**. Effective mentoring requires roughly 60% initiative from the mentee and 40% from the mentor. When mentors shoulder all responsibility for scheduling and follow-up, they signal that the relationship matters more to them than to the mentee - a fundamentally unworkable dynamic.

Exercise: Momentum diagnostic: Early warning system

Use this diagnostic monthly to catch momentum problems before they become relationship problems. Rate each statement from 1 (strongly disagree) to 5 (strongly agree):

Engagement Indicators:	
	Our last meeting ended with specific commitments from both parties
	The mentee initiates contact at least 40% of the time
	We both arrive prepared with topics for discussion
	The mentee demonstrates evidence of action between sessions
	Our conversations go deeper than surface-level updates
Connection Indicators:	
	The mentee shares authentic challenges, not just successes
	I see evidence that the mentee values and applies our discussions
	We reference previous conversations naturally
	Meetings rarely get rescheduled or canceled
	Our conversations feel energizing, not draining
Progress Indicators:	

	I can identify concrete developments in the mentee's situation
	The mentee articulates how they're applying new approaches
	Our focus areas are evolving based on their growth
	Both parties can explain the relationship's current purpose
	The mentee reports specific benefits from our mentoring
	Total

Scoring:

- **60-75 points**: Excellent momentum, maintain current approach
- **45-59 points**: Moderate momentum, proactively discuss patterns before drift sets in
- **30-44 points**: Warning zone, schedule an explicit conversation about relationship health
- **Below 30**: Critical intervention needed: consider whether to reset, restructure, or end

Any individual item scoring 1-2 deserves immediate attention, regardless of overall score. These aren't merely preference mismatches; they're structural problems undermining the relationship's foundation.

Monitoring progress

Everyone is busy! It can be hard to fit the mentoring role into your list of priorities. Similarly, your mentee may also be finding it difficult to make time to reflect on the mentoring opportunity. Time management and commitment to the mentoring process are topics you and the mentee should address regularly and candidly.

As a mentor, some tips to maintain the momentum might include:

- ☐ **Come prepared**

  Learn as much as you can about the mentee before your initial meeting. Before each interaction, ask your mentee what topics or questions they might want to raise. Before each interaction, give yourself 10 or 15 minutes to review what you and the mentee want to discuss and to prepare an agenda.

- ☐ **Talk about the 'big picture.'**

  What are you observing as critical issues for the organization? Offer your strategic insights. Also, if you are able, recount your own experience mentoring (both as a mentor and as a mentee). Explain what worked for you and what didn't.

- ☐ **Active listening**

  Ask questions (you have two ears and one mouth – use them in proportion!) Use open-ended questions. Check understanding frequently ("*Are you saying that…*").

- ☐ **Seek mutual agreement on goals & expectations**

  Explain what you can and cannot provide. Similarly, encourage the mentee to be honest and open about what they can and cannot undertake due to time constraints.

- ☐ **Set a timetable**

  "Let's work on this for 1 month, then we will review progress and see how we should proceed."

☐ **Agree on meeting times and who will set them**

Both the mentor and the mentee should confirm their availability on their respective calendars. Be clear about who 'drives' the schedule and proposes dates, times, durations, venues, and topics.

☐ **Insist on confidentiality**

Mentoring requires trust that what is said between the mentor and mentee remains confidential. Nothing should be divulged to any other parties unless both the mentor and mentee agree.

☐ **Agree to be candid**

Frequent reviews of the relationship should be timetabled. If the relationship is not producing the results you or your mentee expects, that needs to be addressed.

Debrief

Here is the thing about mentoring momentum: it dies quietly, like a houseplant you swore you'd water regularly. You glance over one day and think, "*When did that happen?*" The answer, of course, is gradually, and then suddenly. Most mentoring relationships don't end in dramatic flame-outs; they simply fade into that awkward space where you're both meaning to schedule something but somehow three months have passed, and now it feels weird to reach out.

The good news? Momentum problems are entirely preventable, which means you can stop them before you're reduced to sending apologetic "we should really catch up sometime" messages that both parties know will never materialize. Lally and Gardner's research on habit formation tells us why monthly meetings work better than sporadic marathon sessions: your brain loves patterns in stable contexts. Six-monthly conversations build relationship infrastructure; three intensive sessions followed by a four-month gap just build guilt.

The diagnostic tool isn't an academic exercise; it's your relationship smoke detector. If you're scoring in the warning zone (30-44 points), the building is not on fire yet, but something's definitely smoldering. Address it now with a straightforward conversation or wait six weeks and find yourself essentially starting over, wondering why mentoring feels so exhausting. The five momentum killers all share one trait: they're perfectly fixable through honest discussion, yet we avoid these conversations as if they were performance reviews we forgot to prepare for.

Remember the skilled improviser principle? What works brilliantly in month one might be completely wrong by month six. Strong mentors adapt as relationships mature, adjusting frequency, changing formats, shifting focus, rather than clinging to "this is how we've always done it" while the relationship slowly asphyxiates under the weight of an unchanging routine.

Your next step: Pull out that diagnostic and score your current mentoring relationships. Yes, all of them. Yes, right now. Find your lowest-scoring item and schedule a conversation, not a crisis intervention, just a check-in, to address it explicitly. Try something like: "How's this working for you? What would make our time together more useful?" You'll be amazed how often mentees have been thinking the exact same thing but assumed you were perfectly happy with how things are going. Most momentum problems evaporate once you're both willing to name them. The alternative is watching your relationship drift into that special purgatory of "we really should meet up, " while neither of you believes it will happen.

15. Giving feedback

The feedback sandwich: why two slices of praise don't make the filling disappear

TL;DR

Most managers think they give better feedback than they do. Most mentors do the same. A mentoring relationship provides conditions for honest, developmental feedback that rarely exist elsewhere. The question is whether you are using those conditions well, or replicating the vague, positive feedback habits you have been getting away with since you became a manager. This chapter covers what must be in place before feedback is delivered. There is also an honest discussion of what your mentee is probably not telling you.

Why feedback matters

Most managers have a complicated relationship with feedback. They know it matters, they know they should give it more often, and yet, somehow, it keeps getting deferred, softened, or quietly abandoned. A survey by Zenger & Folkman (2014) found that 44% of managers reported finding it stressful and difficult to give negative feedback, and over a third admitted they avoided the conversation altogether when they anticipated a defensive reaction.[111] This is not a fringe finding. It reflects a deeply embedded discomfort that even experienced leaders who can negotiate contracts, manage crises, and deliver difficult news to stakeholders without flinching can experience.

The mentoring relationship changes this equation (*or it should*). Unlike a performance review, which arrives pre-loaded with institutional weight, career implications, and the shadow of the organization's expectations, feedback in a mentoring context can be given in conditions that rarely exist elsewhere: trust built over time, no hidden agenda, no box to tick, and no performance rating to justify. Ragins and Verbos (2007) describe high-quality mentoring relationships as "relational mentoring": characterized by mutual learning, psychological safety, and genuine care for the other person's development.[112] In those conditions,

---

[111] Zenger, J. and Folkman, J. 2014. "Your Employees Want the Negative Feedback You Hate to Give." *Harvard Business Review*, January.

[112] Ragins, B. R. and Verbos, A. K. 2007. Positive relationships in action: Relational mentoring and mentoring schemas in the workplace. In Ragins, B. R. and Kram, K. E. (Eds.), *The Handbook of Mentoring at Work: Theory, Research, and Practice*. SAGE Publications, 295–318.

feedback lands differently. It can be heard rather than defended against.

Relational mentoring

Consider a mentor who notices that her mentee consistently underplays his contributions in team meetings: deferring to colleagues, qualifying his own ideas, and attributing successes to the group even when his thinking clearly drove the outcome. In a performance review, this might never surface. But a mentor who has met with this person eight or ten times, and who has built enough trust that he admits his anxieties rather than just reporting his achievements, is in a position to name what she sees: "*I've noticed that when you talk about the Henderson project, you say 'the team decided', but last month you told me it was your recommendation that changed the direction. Why do you think you do that?*" That question, asked in that relationship, is worth more than a dozen competency ratings on a feedback form.

Accumulated, trust-based observation matters because the quality of feedback a person receives throughout their career directly affects their development. Hattie & Timperley's (2007) review of over 500 meta-analyses concluded that feedback is among the most powerful influences on learning and performance, but only when it is specific, timely, and perceived as credible. [113] "Specific" and "timely" are qualities that a mentoring relationship can deliver far more consistently than an annual appraisal. "Credible" is where the mentor's experience and investment in the relationship become decisive. A mentee who trusts their mentor and knows the mentor's observations come

---

[113] Hattie, J. and Timperley, H. 2007. "The power of feedback." *Review of Educational Research* 77, no. 1: 81–112.

from experience rather than corporate obligation is far more likely to take feedback seriously and act on it.

There is also a subtler point worth noting. In most organizational settings, honest feedback moves upward only with great difficulty. Junior colleagues rarely tell senior leaders what they think of their decisions, leadership style, or blind spots, not because such observations don't exist, but because the risks of speaking up seem disproportionate. Edmondson's extensive research on psychological safety (1999), further developed in 2018, shows that people consistently withhold feedback, concerns, and ideas when they perceive the environment as unsafe for candor.[114] A well-functioning mentoring relationship can create a genuinely different environment: one where both parties can state what they observe, ask what they don't understand, and receive honest responses without either person's position being threatened.

None of this happens automatically. A mentoring relationship that simply replicates the feedback habits most managers have already learned, vague, infrequent, heavily positive, and delivered only when performance has visibly slipped, wastes the opportunity entirely. The aim of this chapter is to help you use that opportunity well: to give feedback that your mentee can use, to receive feedback that makes you a better mentor and leader, and to build a relationship where honest exchange becomes the norm rather than the exception.

---

[114] Edmondson, A. C. 1999. "Psychological safety and learning behavior in work teams." *Administrative Science Quarterly* 44, no. 2: 350–383. See also Edmondson, A. C. 2018. *The Fearless Organization: Creating Psychological Safety in the Workplace for Learning, Innovation, and Growth.* Wiley.

Creating the right conditions

Even the most well-intentioned feedback, delivered with care and precision, can fail completely if the conditions aren't right. Three conditions are worth considering before a single word of feedback is delivered.

The first is timing within the relationship. Feedback requires a foundation of trust, and trust takes time. Kram's research on mentoring phases (1985) identified the initiation phase, typically the first six to twelve months, as a period focused primarily on building rapport, with more direct developmental challenges becoming appropriate only as the relationship matures.[115] Calibrate the depth and directness of your feedback to the stage the relationship has reached, not the stage you feel it should have reached by now. A mentee who does not yet fully trust their mentor's motives will filter candid feedback through a lens of suspicion, regardless of how carefully it is worded.

The second is the physical and psychological setting. A conversation squeezed into fifteen minutes between back-to-back meetings, conducted in an open-plan office with notifications pinging, is not a feedback conversation: it is a performance of one. Feedback requires the mentee to lower their defenses, sit with an uncomfortable observation, and make sense of it. Steelman & Rutkowski (2004) found that the perceived quality of the feedback environment, privacy, absence of interruptions, the mentor's apparent attentiveness, was a significant predictor of

---

[115] Kram, K.E. 1985. Mentoring at Work: Developmental Relationships in Organizational Life. Scott Foresman.

whether feedback was accepted and used.[116] A private space, adequate time, and a physical arrangement that signals dialogue rather than evaluation are not trivial details.

The third, and perhaps most overlooked, is whether the feedback has been invited. London & Smither (2002) found that individuals who actively sought feedback were significantly more likely to use it for development than those who received it unsolicited.[117] In practice, this doesn't mean waiting to be asked. It means that before offering an observation the mentee hasn't requested, a brief check-in is worth the ten seconds it takes: "*I've noticed something I'd like to share with you, would that be useful*?" That small courtesy signals respect. It preserves the mentee's sense of agency and significantly increases the chances that what follows will land. It is also worth reading the room before proceeding: someone who arrives visibly stressed or preoccupied with a crisis is unlikely to process developmental feedback productively. Sometimes the most useful thing a mentor can do is set the planned agenda aside entirely and simply listen.

---

[116] Steelman, L.A. & Rutkowski, K.A. 2004. "Moderators of employee reactions to negative feedback." *Journal of Managerial Psychology* 19, no. 1: 6–18.

[117] London, M. & Smither, J.W. 2002. "Feedback orientation, feedback culture, and the longitudinal performance management process." *Human Resource Management Review* 12, no. 1: 81–100.

What your mentee is not telling you

One of the more underused tools in a mentor's repertoire is simply asking the mentee, directly and sincerely: "*How am I doing*?" This sounds straightforward, but it runs counter to a deeply ingrained assumption: that in a mentoring relationship, feedback flows in only one direction. Deliberately inverting that dynamic can be one of the most valuable things a mentor does. Day, Harrison & Halpin (2009) argue that leaders who actively seek feedback from those they lead develop greater self-awareness and are perceived as more credible, precisely because asking signals confidence rather than vulnerability.[118]

A mentee who is genuinely invited to say "*I find it more helpful when you ask questions rather than share your own experience*" is learning something as valuable as any skill their mentor has passed on, that giving honest feedback upward is both possible and worth the discomfort. The mentor benefits too: a candid answer will almost certainly reveal a blind spot that no peer or line manager has mentioned.

The catch is that the invitation must be genuine. A perfunctory "*any feedback for me?*" tacked onto the end of a session while gathering up papers will produce nothing useful. The mentor who pauses, makes eye contact, and says, "*I'd genuinely like to know what I could do differently, take a moment and be honest with me,* " is signaling something quite different. That signal, more than the question itself, is what makes this work.

---

[118] Day, D.V., Harrison, M.M. & Halpin, S.M. 2009. An Integrative Approach to Leader Development: Connecting Adult Development, Identity, and Expertise. Psychology Press

What good feedback looks like: the SBI model

Having the right conditions in place gets feedback into the room. What you say determines whether it stays there. Most feedback fails not because the mentor doesn't care, but because there is no clear structure: the observation meanders, the point gets buried, the mentee isn't sure what they're being asked to reflect on, and the conversation drifts. A simple, research-backed framework resolves this.

The SBI model gives feedback on a reliable three-part structure: Situation, Behavior, Impact. [119] It sounds almost too simple, but its value lies precisely in that simplicity. Each element does a specific job, and together they produce feedback that is specific enough to be actionable, grounded enough to be credible, and bounded enough to avoid the personality judgments that make feedback feel like an attack.

Situation anchors the feedback to a specific, observable moment rather than a generalized impression. "*When you presented to the senior team on Thursday*" is a situation. "*Whenever you're in meetings*" is not an assertion that the mentee is unlikely to accept and will probably dispute. The situation element requires the mentor to have observed something rather than relying on rumors, assumptions, or accumulated impressions.

Behavior describes what was said or done, not what was meant, not what it implies about the mentee's character, not what

---

[119] Centre for Creative Leadership. 2022. T*he SBI™ Feedback Model: Situation-Behavior-Impac*t. See also Weitzel, S. R. 2000. *Feedback That Works: How to Build and Deliver Your Message*. Centre for Creative Leadership Press.

others think about it. "*You interrupted the Finance Director three times before she had finished speaking*" is behavior. "*You were disrespectful*" is an interpretation. This distinction matters enormously. Behavior is observable and therefore harder to deny; interpretation invites an argument about motives that derails the conversation before it has started.

Impact explains the consequences for the team, the mentee's relationships, and the outcome. This is the most frequently omitted element, and its absence is why so much feedback fails to motivate change. Telling someone what they did without explaining why it mattered gives them no reason to do anything differently. "*The Finance Director didn't contribute again after that point, and we lost her input on the budget assumptions*" connects the behavior to a real outcome the mentee can care about.

Putting it together, a piece of SBI feedback might sound like this: *"In Thursday's presentation, the one to the senior team, you interrupted the Finance Director three times before she'd finished her point. After the third time, she stopped contributing to the discussion entirely, and we didn't get her input on the budget assumptions, which I know you needed."* That is specific, observable, and consequential. It is also something the mentee can do something about.

A note on tone: SBI provides the structure, not the warmth. The framework tells you what elements to include - it doesn't dictate how you deliver them. A mentor who recites SBI in a clipped, clinical manner will still produce feedback that feels like a dressing-down. The conditions covered earlier in this chapter, trust, privacy, and the right moment, are what make SBI land as a genuine act of support rather than a structured complaint.

Enhancing feedback effectiveness

Even with a clear framework to hand, there are several predictable ways that feedback goes wrong in practice. Most of them involve departing from the principles that make SBI effective. Although most of us would welcome positive, supportive feedback, there are many examples of thoughtless or limited feedback. Listed below are a few 'warning signs' to be aware of:

The most common feedback failures tend to cluster around a few recurring mistakes. The first focuses on the person rather than on what they did. Feedback about personality, assumed character traits, or inferred motivations is both demotivating and easily rejected; it gives the mentee nothing concrete to work with and often provokes defensiveness. Unless you happen to be a trained psychoanalyst, speculating about why someone behaves as they do is territory best avoided. Stick to what you observed, describe the outcomes, and invite the mentee to reflect on the reasons.

Closely related is the problem of vagueness. If you cannot point to specific, verifiable behavior and its consequences, you do not yet have feedback; you have an opinion. The same applies to generalities: statements like "*behaving like that will always lead to success*" may feel wise in the moment, but offer the mentee nothing actionable. If you find yourself reaching for generalities, it usually signals that you need more direct observation or a development activity that allows the mentee to reach their own conclusions.

Keep it yours, keep it brief

Two further habits undermine feedback even when the content is sound. The first is speaking for others, attributing observations to unnamed colleagues or sharing what you have inferred from the reactions of people who aren't in the room. Feedback carries the most weight when it is grounded in what you personally witnessed. The moment it becomes "people have been saying..." the mentee's attention shifts from reflection to detective work. The second is allowing feedback conversations to run too long. Whether the feedback is positive or developmental, brevity sharpens its impact. If there are several issues worth raising, resist the temptation to address them all at once, prioritize the one or two that are most clearly evidenced and most directly relevant to the mentee's current goals, and return to the others in a subsequent session.

The well-known technique of sandwiching critical feedback between two positive observations deserves a mention, if only to discourage it. Most people who have received feedback in a management context will recognize the approach, and many will have a rather earthier name for it. Recipients instinctively weigh the positive elements more heavily and minimize the developmental ones, precisely the opposite of the intended effect. Address each topic separately, giving each its own space rather than blurring them together in the hope that the positives will soften the landing.

Two habits that are easy to miss

Using humor to ease the tension in a difficult feedback conversation is instinctive; it relaxes the person giving the feedback, at least. The risk is that it rarely has the same effect on the recipient. Exaggerating a behavior for comic effect can land very differently on someone who is already feeling exposed; leave the levity for a more appropriate moment. Framing observations as questions, "*Why did you do that*?", tends to produce defensiveness rather than reflection. State what you observed, then ask the mentee for their response.

The Good, the bad, and the ugly

Here is an example scenario that shows how the same underlying observation can be delivered poorly, adequately, or well. The mentee is a mid-level manager who has recently begun to struggle in cross-functional meetings, becoming visibly dismissive when colleagues from other departments raise concerns about her team's project timelines.

Version 1: Vague and personality-focused

"I've been hearing from a few people that you can come across as a bit difficult in meetings. You need to be more of a team player: people notice these things, and it won't do your reputation any good."

This version fails on almost every count. It attributes the feedback to unnamed third parties rather than to the mentor's own observation, labels the mentee's character rather than describing a specific behavior, offers no concrete example that the mentee can recall or reflect on, and closes with a veiled threat to the mentee's reputation. Most mentees receiving this feedback will spend their energy wondering who said what rather than considering what they might change.

Version 2: Specific but incomplete

"In last Tuesday's cross-functional meeting, when the logistics team raised concerns about the timeline, you said their objections were 'not really relevant to the core project.' That came across as quite dismissive."

This is better. There is a specific situation, and the behavior is described rather than inferred. But it stops short of explaining why it matters: the impact is implied rather than stated, leaving the mentee to guess at the consequences. Some mentees will connect the dots; others will hear this as a one-off observation and conclude that being a little blunter than ideal on one occasion is hardly a significant issue.

Version 3: SBI in full

"In last Tuesday's cross-functional meeting, when the logistics team raised their timeline concerns, you said their objections were 'not really relevant to the core project' and moved on. I watched the logistics lead, she didn't speak again for the rest of the session. Afterwards, I noticed she wasn't included in the follow-up email thread, which suggests the relationship may already be fraying. That team's sign-off is on your critical path. If they feel their input isn't welcome, getting their cooperation when you need it is going to be significantly harder."

The situation is precise. The behavior is observable and specific, not a character judgment, but a thing that was said. The impact operates on two levels: the immediate effect on the room, and the longer-term consequence for the project. The mentee now has a reason to care, not just a reason to feel criticized.

Notice also what Version 3 doesn't do: it doesn't tell the mentee what to do differently, at least not yet. That is deliberate. The mentor's job at this point is to share what was observed and why it matters, then invite reflection: "What's your read on how that landed?" The conversation that follows, where the mentee works through what happened and what she might do next, is where the real development occurs. Handing over a ready-made solution at the end of the feedback short-circuits the entire process.

Exercise: Building a real piece of feedback

PURPOSE

Reading about SBI is one thing; applying it in a real-world situation is another! This exercise walks you through building feedback for your mentee using the Situation–Behavior–Impact structure before you deliver it. Preparing feedback in writing, even briefly, significantly improves its clarity and reduces the risk of slipping into the habits identified in the Feedback habits self-assessment.

INSTRUCTIONS

Think of one observation you have been meaning to share with your mentee, something you have noticed but perhaps not yet found the right way to raise. It can be a development area or a genuine strength that warrants a specific name rather than a vague acknowledgment.

Work through each element below:

SITUATION

Identify the specific occasion you are going to reference. When was it? What was the context? Be precise enough that your mentee will immediately know what you are referring to.

Check: Is this something you directly observed, or something you have inferred or heard from others? If you do not yet have the material for SBI feedback, consider creating a direct observation opportunity first.

BEHAVIOR

Describe, as precisely as possible, what was said or done. Use observable, specific language. Avoid adjectives that describe character ("dismissive", "confident", "aggressive") and instead describe the actual words or actions.

Check: If your mentee disputes this description, would you be able to point to specific, verifiable evidence? If not, soften your language to reflect that this is your perception rather than an objective fact.

IMPACT

What were the consequences of this behavior: on the mentee, on others, on the outcome of the situation, or on the mentee's longer-term goals? Be as specific as possible. Avoid vague statements like "it didn't create a great impression."

Check: Does this impact connect to something the mentee cares about: their goals, their relationships, their reputation, their development? If not, they are unlikely to be sufficiently motivated to act on it.

YOUR OPENING QUESTION

SBI delivers the observation; a well-chosen question opens the dialogue. Write the question you will ask immediately after sharing the feedback, the one that hands the conversation back to the mentee and invites genuine reflection rather than a defensive response.

Examples to consider: "*What's your read on how that landed?*" / "*Does that resonate with you?*" / "*What was going through your mind at that point?*" / "*How does that sit with what you're trying to achieve?*"

NOW READ IT BACK

Read through everything you have written as a continuous piece of feedback. Ask yourself:

- ☐ Would I recognize this situation immediately if I were the mentee?
- ☐ Is there anything here that describes character rather than behavior?
- ☐ Is the impact specific enough to be motivating?
- ☐ Does my opening question genuinely invite reflection, or does it lead the mentee towards my conclusion?

Adjust anything that doesn't pass those four tests before your next meeting.

Debrief

Most people in leadership roles believe they handle feedback reasonably well, right up until they examine their actual habits closely.

The conditions that a good mentoring relationship creates, accumulated trust, no institutional agenda, and genuine investment in the other person's development, are rare in organizational life. Most people receive feedback that is too vague to act on, too infrequent to build on, and too carefully softened to be honest. A mentor who uses those conditions well is offering something most organizations cannot.

The SBI model will not do that work on its own. Tone, timing, and relationship matter just as much as structure. What SBI removes are the most common structural failures: the generalities, the personality judgments, the feedback that leaves the mentee with no clear reason to change. Get the structure right, and the conversation has a chance. Get it wrong, and even the best intentions produce defensiveness.

The section on openness to feedback deserves a final thought. Senior leaders rarely receive honest developmental input from those around them, not because it doesn't exist, but because the power dynamics make candor feel risky. A mentee who has been genuinely invited to share what they think, and who has watched their mentor receive that feedback without flinching, has learned something that will serve them throughout their career. You are not just giving feedback in this relationship. You are modeling what it looks like to seek it, receive it, and use it in a useful way.

Your next step: Before your next mentoring session, complete the SBI preparation exercise, write out one observation you have been meaning to raise but haven't yet found the right way to deliver. Then, at the end of that same session, ask your mentee directly: "Is there anything I could do differently that would make our conversations more useful?" Sit with whatever answer you receive without explaining, justifying, or qualifying. You will have practiced both sides of this chapter in a single meeting.

16. Managing the transition

All good things must end (and a few mediocre ones too)

TL;DR:

Most mentoring relationships do not end; they simply stop. Sessions become less frequent, action items go unreviewed, and both parties drift without ever formally acknowledging that the work is done. It is the relational equivalent of leaving a party without saying goodbye: easier in the moment, mildly unsatisfying for everyone. This chapter argues that endings deserve better. Plan for the close from the beginning. Watch for the signals that the relationship has run its course: goals achieved, conversations grown shallow, calendars mysteriously always full. A good ending is the last thing a mentee remembers. Make it count.

Why endings matter

There is a natural human tendency to treat the conclusion of a mentoring relationship as an afterthought, something that happens *to* the relationship rather than something you actively manage. Meetings become less frequent, agendas grow thinner, and eventually one party sends a message saying, "*We really must catch up,* " that neither of them acts on. The relationship doesn't end; it simply evaporates.

This matters more than most mentors realize. Kram's research on mentoring phases established that the "separation" stage, when the formal relationship begins to wind down, is not a passive event but an active developmental opportunity in its own right.[120] Handled well, it consolidates the mentee's growth and reinforces their readiness to operate independently. Handled poorly, it leaves both parties with a vague sense of unfinished business and a slightly awkward encounter every time they pass in the corridor.

The psychological research on how people remember experiences adds further weight to this argument. Kahneman's peak-end rule demonstrates that we evaluate experiences primarily through two lenses: their most intense moment and their ending.[121] The quality of everything in between, however good, carries less weight in memory than the final impression. A two-year mentoring relationship of genuine value can be subtly undermined by a conclusion that simply fizzles out. A deliberate

---

[120] Kram, K.E. 1985. Mentoring at Work: Developmental Relationships in Organizational Life. Scott Foresman

[121] Kahneman, D., Fredrickson, B.L., Schreiber, C.A. & Redelmeier, D.A. 1993. "When more pain is preferred to less: Adding a better end." *Psychological Science* 4, no. 6: 401–405.

and positive closure, by contrast, can leave both parties with a stronger sense of what was achieved, even if the journey had its rough patches.

There is also a practical dimension. Research by Ragins and Kram found that mentors who managed relationship endings well were significantly more likely to take on new mentees in the future, and to do so with greater confidence and skill.[122] In other words, how you close one relationship shapes how well you open the next. Endings, it turns out, are not separate from the mentoring process. They are part of it.

Putting peak-end into practice

Kahneman's research on how people remember experiences produced one of the more counterintuitive findings in behavioral psychology: we do not remember experiences as an average of how they felt throughout. Instead, our memories are disproportionately shaped by two moments: the most emotionally intense point of the experience and its ending. Everything in between, however long or rich, contributes surprisingly little to how we benefit.[123] Kahneman called this *the peak-end rule,* and its implications for mentoring are direct. A relationship that was largely positive but ended badly will be remembered as largely negative. In contrast, a relationship that had its difficulties but closed with genuine care and reflection will leave both parties with a memory that does justice to the work they did together.

---

[122] Ragins, B.R. & Kram, K.E. 2007. The Handbook of Mentoring at Work: Theory, Research and Practice. Sage Publications

[123] Kahneman, D., Fredrickson, B.L., Schreiber, C.A. & Redelmeier, D.A. 1993. "When more pain is preferred to less: Adding a better end." *Psychological Science* 4, no. 6: 401–405

The practical implication is not that mentors should stage-manage their exits. It is simply that endings deserve deliberate attention. As the relationship approaches its close, four things are worth considering:

- ✓ **Begin with the end in mind.** At the outset, explore anticipated outcomes with your mentee. What measures of success might be relevant? Revisit those measures as the relationship progresses.
- ✓ **Review progress.** Look back on the entire journey together. Ask your mentee to initiate this review. What went well, and what didn't? If specific measures of success were agreed at the outset, review what occurred.
- ✓ **Celebrate success**. Identify achievements and milestones. Recognize the contribution of each of you.
- ✓ **Discuss what's next**. How should the relationship evolve? How will your mentee identify future mentors? Are there opportunities for them to become mentors to others?

The sections that follow explore each of these in more depth.

Recognizing the signals

A jazz musician does not stop playing because the clock says so. They stop because they can hear that the music has arrived somewhere: the phrase has resolved, the energy has shifted, the piece has said what it needed to say. Knowing when to end is as much a skill as knowing how to play.

Mentoring relationships work much the same way. Clutterbuck's five-phase model identifies "winding up" and "moving on" as a gradual progression, typically characterized by reduced learning intensity, increased mentee autonomy, and a natural shift in the emotional tone of conversations.[124] The signals tend to fall into three categories, each requiring a different response.

Natural completion is the most satisfying. The goals established at the outset have been met, confidence has grown visibly, and the mentee is increasingly bringing answers to sessions rather than questions. When a mentee routinely solves their own problems before they arrive, that is not a failure of the relationship: it is its success. The diagnostic question is simple: Is this relationship still stretching them, or has it become a comfort?

Circumstantial change is external and often sudden: a role change, a restructure, a relocation, a promotion. The mentor's experience may no longer be directly relevant; the mentee's needs may have moved beyond what this relationship can offer. These signals are usually obvious. What is less obvious, and what mentors often avoid, is the honest conversation about whether the relationship should adapt, pause, or conclude.

Relationship drift is the trickiest category and the most important to catch early. Unlike the others, it has no clear external cause; it simply happens when neither party actively tends to the relationship. Sessions are rescheduled more often than held; the mentee arrives without a clear agenda; conversations become pleasant but shallow. Crucially, drift feels comfortable. Nobody is unhappy. Nobody is doing anything wrong. The relationship is just coasting.

The risk is that drift can persist for months without either party addressing it, because addressing it requires someone to say something slightly awkward. The mentor is well placed to say

---

[124] Clutterbuck, D. 2014. *Everyone Needs a Mentor* (5th ed.). London: CIPD.

it first: "I've noticed our conversations have felt a bit less focused recently: is that just me, or are you feeling it too?" opens the door without drama.

A useful self-check before each session: What does my mentee need from me right now that they couldn't get elsewhere? If the honest answer is "not much, " the relationship may be sending a signal worth heeding.

Beginning with the end in mind

Stephen Covey's instruction to "begin with the end in mind" risks becoming clichéd,[125] but there is a reason it endures. If you and your mentee never define what success looks like, you will have no meaningful way to recognize it when it arrives, and no agreed basis on which to decide that the relationship has run its course. A relationship that begins with "let's see how it goes" will almost certainly conclude with "well, it sort of fizzled out."

Locke and Latham's work on goal-setting theory is unambiguous: specific, challenging goals consistently produce better outcomes than open-ended intentions.[126] The principle translates directly; relationships with clearly defined objectives give both parties a shared reference point, something to work towards and to return to when the question of transition arises.

In practice, this means having a genuine conversation in your first or second meeting about what the mentee hopes to achieve and what the mentor can reasonably offer. The outcomes don't

---

[125] Covey, S.R. 1989. The 7 Habits of Highly Effective People: Powerful Lessons in Personal Change. New York: Free Press

[126] Locke, E.A. & Latham, G.P. 2002. “Building a practically useful theory of goal setting and task motivation: A 35-year odyssey.” *American Psychologist 57, no. 9: 705–717.*

need to be rigidly quantified; mentoring is not a performance management process, but they should be specific enough to be recognizable. "I *want to feel more confident in executive-level meetings*" is more useful than "*I want to develop as a leader.*" "*I'd like to have a clearer sense of whether to apply for a director role in the next twelve months,* " gives the relationship a natural horizon.

These initial agreements serve a dual purpose. In the early stages, they provide direction. In the later stages, they provide the basis for an honest review. A mentor who can point back to what was agreed at the outset, and invite the mentee to assess where they now stand, is in a far stronger position to have a productive closing conversation than one who must reconstruct the relationship's purpose from memory.

Two practical points. First, revisit the success criteria periodically; what mattered at month three may look quite different at month eighteen. Treating initial goals as fixed rather than as a working document is a mistake. Second, make sure the criteria address both the mentor and the mentee. Mentoring is a two-way relationship, and asking yourself, "*What am I hoping to gain from this?*" at the outset is not self-interested; it is honest, and honesty at the start makes for cleaner conversations at the end.

Closing review – Looking back together

The final session of a mentoring relationship deserves more than a handshake and a promise to stay in touch. It is an often-missed opportunity to consolidate what has been learned, acknowledge what has been achieved, and give both parties a proper sense of completion.

The case for structured reflection rests on solid ground. Kolb's model of experiential learning argues that experience alone does not produce learning; reflection converts experience into knowledge. Without it, even the richest mentoring journey can leave both parties unclear about what they gained. The closing review is that reflection, deliberately built rather than left to chance.

Three areas provide a useful structure. First, looking back: what were the original goals, and what happened to them? Some will have been achieved, others will have shifted, and a few may have been quietly abandoned when they turned out to be the wrong goals. Acknowledging this honestly is more valuable than curating a neat success narrative. Second, identifying the turning points: which conversations or moments of insight made the biggest difference? Asking the mentee to name two or three interventions gives the mentor useful feedback on which ones landed. Third, naming the learning: what does the mentee now know, believe, or do differently? This is distinct from listing achievements; it attempts to articulate the internal shifts that underpin them. A mentee might have secured a promotion by learning to assert their views in senior meetings without apologizing for taking up space. Both matter, but it is the learning that travels to the next role.

The closing review is not solely for the mentee's benefit. Effective mentors treat it as professional development: what did you do well in this relationship, and what would you do differently?

A practical note on timing: the closing review works best when explicitly named as such at the start of the final session, not added as an afterthought. Ask the mentee in advance to bring answers to three questions: What are you most proud of? What was hardest? What will you carry forward? These ensure the review begins with the mentee's voice, exactly where it should.

Celebrating the journey

There is often a tendency to underplay achievement. Acknowledge what went well, and someone will point out what could have gone better. In mentoring, this instinct toward modesty can quietly undermine one of the most valuable things a closing session can do: give both parties genuine permission to recognize what they have accomplished together.

Celebration here does not mean bunting and a cake (though nobody is stopping you). It means deliberately pausing to name progress, acknowledge effort, and mark the transition with the seriousness it deserves. Amabile and Kramer found that the single most powerful motivator at work was a sense of making progress, and that recognition of that progress amplified its effect considerably. Achievement that goes unacknowledged registers less deeply, both emotionally and motivationally.

The most meaningful acknowledgment is usually the most specific. Generic praise, "*you've done really well*", lands softly and fades quickly. Specific recognition of concrete growth is different in kind: "*You walked into this relationship convinced you couldn't chair difficult meetings. You chaired three in the last six months, and each time you handled the pushback more confidently than the last.*" That kind of observation requires the mentor to have been paying attention throughout, which is itself a mark of the relationship's quality.

It also helps to distinguish between two objects of celebration: the outcomes, goals achieved, challenges navigated, and the process, the courage it took to show up honestly and examine uncomfortable assumptions. A mentee who achieved modest external results but developed real self-awareness deserves recognition for that inner work just as much as one who secured a promotion.

Finally, there is value in the mentor acknowledging what the relationship gave them. A few sentences after the final session, noting how far the mentee has come, cost very little to write and are rarely forgotten.

What comes next – for both of you

Ending the formal relationship does not mean ending the relationship. Many mentors and mentees assume, without ever discussing it, that the conclusion of a structured program marks the end of the connection. It rarely does, and forcing a clean break where a natural evolution is possible is usually the wrong instinct.

What tends to happen instead is a gradual transition from one kind of relationship to another. Johnson's research identified this shift as one of the defining features of mentoring relationships that end well: the hierarchical, developmental dynamic gives way to something more collegial, a professional friendship characterized by mutual respect and occasional contact rather than regular structured support.[127] What remains, when the relationship has gone well, is a durable connection between two people who know each other's working minds reasonably well.

This evolution should be discussed, not assumed. One of the more useful conversations in the closing session is a brief, direct one about what each party would like to see going forward. Some mentees will want periodic contact: a check-in every few months, a message when something significant happens. Others will prefer a cleaner break, not from indifference but because

---

[127] Johnson, W.B. 2007. On Being a Mentor: A Guide for Higher Education Faculty. Lawrence Erlbaum Associates.

they associate continued contact with continued dependence. Both are reasonable. The mistake is leaving it unspoken, creating an ambiguous limbo where neither party is sure whether reaching out would be welcome or intrusive.

It is also worth helping the mentee consider their wider support structures. Higgins & Kram argued that the most resilient professionals cultivate a developmental network: a portfolio of connections that together provide the challenge, support, and perspective that no single mentor can offer.[128] The end of a mentoring relationship is a natural moment to prompt this thinking: who else are they learning from, and are there gaps worth filling? That is not a diminishment of what you have built together. It is the point.

For the mentor, this relationship becomes part of an evolving practice. The patterns you noticed, the interventions that worked, the moments where you adjusted: all of it carries forward into the next relationship, and the one after that.

When endings go badly

Not every mentoring relationship ends with a closing review and a warm handshake. Some end in confusion, some in disappointment, and a few in something both parties would rather not examine too closely.

Scandura's early work on dysfunctional mentoring identified three recurring patterns that tend to lead to poor outcomes: mentors who become overly controlling, treating the mentee's development as an extension of their own agenda; relationships

---

[128] Higgins, M.C. & Kram, K.E. 2001. "Reconceptualizing mentoring at work: A developmental network perspective." *Academy of Management Review* 26, no. 2: 264–288.

characterized by neglect, where the mentor's engagement fades without explanation; and sabotage - rare but real. Most difficult endings involve one of the first two: a relationship that became unhelpfully dependent, or one that simply ran out of oxygen.[129]

Premature endings deserve particular attention. A relationship that ends before the mentee's goals are met, through a mentor's departure, a change in circumstances, or a loss of trust, can leave the mentee feeling abandoned or confirmed in a belief that support is unreliable. Eby et al. found that negative mentoring experiences, including abrupt endings, were associated not only with reduced satisfaction but with a diminished willingness to seek mentoring support in the future. A badly handled ending does not merely disappoint; it can close doors the mentee may not realize they have shut.[130]

When an ending is going badly, the instinct is often to minimize. This instinct is understandable and usually wrong. A direct, brief conversation, "*I think we've both noticed that our sessions have lost momentum; it might be worth talking about where we are*", gives both parties a chance to either recalibrate or close with some dignity intact.

A relationship that ended badly is, among other things, data. The skilled improviser does not ignore the performance that went wrong; they study it more carefully than the ones that went well.

---

[129] Scandura, T.A. 1998. "Dysfunctional mentoring relationships and outcomes." *Journal of Management 24, no. 3: 449–467.*

[130] Eby, L.T., McManus, S.E., Simon, S.A. & Russell, J.E.A. 2000. "The protégé's perspective regarding negative mentoring experiences: The development of a taxonomy." *Journal of Vocational Behavior* 57, no. 1: 1–21

Finally, a practical note: if you are operating within a formal mentoring program, a difficult or premature ending should be reported to whoever coordinates it, not for blame or bureaucratic process, but to ensure the mentee has access to alternative support and to provide the organization with the information it needs to improve future pairings. Staying silent to avoid awkwardness serves no one.

Debrief

Endings are the part of mentoring that practitioners most consistently undervalue. Research shows that how a relationship closes shapes how both parties remember it, and, for mentees, whether they seek mentoring support again in the future. The winding-down stage deserves the same intentionality that good mentors bring to goal-setting and feedback, not a hasty goodbye at the end of an overrunning session.

The practical implications are straightforward. Plan for the ending from the beginning. Watch for the signals. Use the final session to review, reflect, and celebrate, not because it is a nice thing to do, but because structured reflection is what converts experience into learning. If things have not gone well, have the honest conversation anyway. Silence rarely improves a difficult situation; it just leaves both parties to interpret it privately, usually less charitably than the truth warrants.

Your next step: Before your next mentoring session, ask yourself one question: if this relationship were to end today, would you both leave knowing what had been achieved, what had been learned, and what the other person meant to the journey? If the answer is anything less than a confident yes, you have work to do. The good news is that it is not complicated work. It just requires the one thing that all good mentors have in plentiful supply: the willingness to pay attention.

17. Mentoring in a changing world

Mentoring in your pajamas: A professional guide

TL;DR

The world your mentee works in has changed in ways that matter for mentoring. Hybrid and remote working have stripped out the informal developmental texture that in-person offices once provided for free: the corridor conversations, the accidental visibility, the chance encounters that quietly shaped careers. Structured mentoring now compensates for much of what used to happen without anyone having to arrange it. The core skills travel well across a screen; what changes is the effort required to make them land. And then there is AI, which your mentee is almost certainly already using, and probably not telling you about.

The world your mentee is working in

Something quietly significant happened to workplace development during the pandemic, and it hasn't fully reversed. When offices emptied out in 2020, organizations lost something they had never thought to measure: the informal, unscheduled, accidental side of professional development. The hallway conversation with a senior colleague. The spontaneous debrief after a difficult client meeting. The coffee queue exchange that turned into career advice nobody had planned to give. None of this appeared on any learning and development budget, yet it was doing enormous work.

Yang et al., analyzing communication data from over 60,000 Microsoft employees, found that remote work significantly weakened "weak ties", the loose connections between colleagues who don't work closely together but who are often the source of new ideas, opportunities, and introductions. Professional networks became more siloed, with collaboration concentrated among people who already worked closely together.[131] For early- and mid-career professionals, these weak ties are where much of the informal mentoring happens. When they frayed, structured mentoring became one of the few remaining mechanisms through which that development could occur.

Your mentee, depending on their role and organization, may now spend most of their working week in a home office, a coffee shop, or a hybrid arrangement that puts them in a building two or three days a week without any guarantee of encountering the

---

[131] Yang, L., Holtz, D., Jaffe, S., Suri, S., Sinha, S., Weston, J., Joyce, C., Shah, N., Sherman, K., Hecht, B., & Teevan, J. 2022. "The effects of remote work on collaboration among information workers." *Nature Human Behavior* 6, no. 1: 43–54.

right people. They may be technically visible, on Slack, on Teams, on email, whilst being professionally invisible in the ways that drive career progression: being seen handling a difficult situation well, being overheard contributing in a meeting, being noticed by people three levels above them who would otherwise never have had cause to register their existence.

This matters because it shifts what the mentoring relationship needs to do. Historically, a mentor provided perspective, challenge, and the occasional well-placed introduction. Today, the relationship is also compensating for the developmental texture of a working environment that has simply become thinner. That is not a criticism of hybrid working; the evidence on its benefits is substantial. It is simply a reality worth naming, because a mentor who understands it will approach the relationship differently.

What changes in a virtual or hybrid relationship

The first thing most mentors notice when they move a relationship online is that it feels slightly harder to read the room. In a face-to-face conversation, you pick up information continuously: posture, eye contact, the small hesitation before an answer, the way someone's energy shifts when a topic makes them uncomfortable. On a video call, you get a fraction of that. On an audio call, less still. This isn't a reason to avoid virtual mentoring; it is simply a reason to work a little harder at the things that in-person settings provided automatically.

Rapport is the first casualty of distance. Breuer et al. found that trust matters significantly more in virtual relationships than in face-to-face ones, not just harder to build, but more consequential when it's absent.[132] In a physical office, a mentoring relationship can survive a patch of low trust because other interactions fill the gap. Virtually, those accidental repairs don't happen. If trust erodes, there is nothing to catch it. The early sessions of a virtual relationship, therefore, deserve more deliberate investment in getting to know each other. Resist the temptation to get straight down to business; the small talk you might abbreviate in person is doing structural work online.

The "out of sight, out of mind" problem is real and worth acknowledging directly. In a physical office, a mentor naturally stays aware of their mentee's situation: they see them in meetings, hear about projects through colleagues, and notice when something seems off. Virtually, that ambient awareness disappears almost entirely. You know only what your mentee tells you, which means you are dependent on them being sufficiently self-aware and forthcoming to surface the things that matter. Some mentees are, many are not. Compensating for this requires more deliberate check-in questions at the start of sessions: not just "*how are things going?*" but "*what's happened since we last spoke that I should know about?*"

A specific challenge arises in hybrid arrangements, where one party is in an office, and the other is remote. This asymmetry can subtly distort the relationship. The in-office person has a richer organizational context: they know the mood in the building, what conversations are happening informally, and which

---

[132] Breuer, C., Hüffmeier, J., & Hertel, G. 2016. "Does trust matter more in virtual teams? A meta-analysis of trust and team effectiveness considering virtuality and documentation as moderators." *Journal of Applied Psychology* 101, no. 8: 1151–1177.

way the political wind is blowing. The remote person may be working from a significantly thinner picture of reality. Good mentors in this situation actively share that contextual information rather than assuming their mentee already has it.

Finally, there is the question of session structure. Virtual meetings have a different energy from in-person ones: they are more tiring, more easily interrupted, and harder to sustain across a full hour. Shorter, more frequent sessions often work better than longer, less frequent ones in a virtual context. A 40-minute call every three weeks will typically outperform a 90-minute call every six weeks, both in maintaining momentum and keeping the relationship feeling alive rather than transactional.

What doesn't change

It is easy to conclude that the whole enterprise is fundamentally different when conducted remotely. It isn't. The setting changes; the substance doesn't.

Every core skill covered in this book, listening carefully, asking questions that open rather than close, giving feedback that lands, holding a mentee accountable without tipping into management, works the same way on a video call as it does across a coffee table. Decades of evidence consistently point to the same qualities: genuine interest in the mentee's development, honest conversation, and a willingness to both challenge and support. None of that has an asterisk saying, "applies only in person."

What changes is the effort required to deploy those skills. Reading a mentee's emotional state takes more deliberate attention when you can only see their face in a small rectangle on a screen. Creating psychological safety, the condition in which a mentee feels genuinely safe to raise concerns, admit uncertainty, or push back on your advice, requires more explicit signaling when you can't rely on body language and physical presence to communicate warmth. A 2023 review of psychological safety research confirmed that trust-building behaviors need to be more actively and visibly demonstrated in remote settings, where the ambient signals of a shared physical environment are simply absent.[133] Holding silence, one of the most powerful tools in a mentor's repertoire, feels more awkward on a video call, where both parties are conditioned to fill gaps quickly to avoid appearing to have a frozen connection.

The skilled improviser's task in a virtual or hybrid context is therefore not to learn new skills, but to apply familiar ones with greater intentionality.

The core skills: What works and what does not in different contexts
(Adapted from the mentor competency framework in Chapter 5)

Skill	What stays the same	What requires more effort
Active listening	The goal: full attention on your mentee	Harder without physical cues, watch facial micro-expressions closely
Questioning	Open questions work identically	Silence after a question feels more awkward; hold it anyway
Feedback	SBI model applies unchanged	Delivering difficult feedback needs even more careful scene-setting

[133] Edmondson, A.C. & Bransby, D.P. 2023. "Psychological safety comes of age: Observed themes in an established literature." *Annual Review of Organizational Psychology and Organizational Behavior* 10: 55–78.

Trust-building	Consistency and honesty remain the foundation	Must be built more deliberately without incidental contact
Accountability	Agreed actions, reviewed at each session	Follow-up needs to be more structured; nothing happens by accident

AI as a new presence in the mentoring relationship

Something has quietly compounded the challenge of remote mentoring, a challenge that most guides to virtual working have yet to address. Your remote mentee already faces one invisibility problem: they are not in the building, so they are not being seen handling difficult situations, contributing to meetings, or demonstrating the kind of judgment that gets noticed by people three levels above them. But there is a second invisibility problem alongside it, and together they create something more challenging than either alone.

Since late 2022, most knowledge workers have incorporated AI tools into their daily working practice to some degree. For remote workers, the adoption rate has been particularly high: when you are working alone, with no colleague to turn to for a quick sense-check, an AI tool that produces a confident, well-structured response in thirty seconds is genuinely useful. The result is that your mentee's visible work product, the documents, analyses, and recommendations they produce, may look more polished than the thinking behind them is. And in a remote setting, you have very little else to go on.

Research by Dell'Acqua et al., based on a field experiment with knowledge workers, found that AI raises the floor for routine tasks dramatically, while leaving the genuinely hard problems: the ambiguous, the politically sensitive, and the ethically complex — entirely to humans![134]

Your mentee is producing better first drafts faster. What is landing on their desk as a result is a higher proportion of the problems that AI cannot touch. A 2026 study found that while employee-AI collaboration frees workers from repetitive tasks, the channel through which tacit knowledge gets transferred (the kind of judgment that only comes from lived experience in a specific context) remained firmly human.[135] AI accelerates output. It does not develop the person producing it.

One practical thing to listen for: a mentee who presents conclusions with great confidence, but whose reasoning becomes thin quite quickly when you probe it. This is not necessarily a sign of intellectual weakness. It may be a sign that the conclusion was generated rather than developed, and that the mentee has not yet done the work of genuinely owning it.

There is also a specific discomfort that has emerged among knowledge workers who use AI regularly, and it is almost never raised openly in professional settings. When your mentee

---

134 Dell'Acqua, F., McFowland III, E., Mollick, E., Lifshitz-Assaf, H., Kellogg, K. C., Rajendran, S., Krayer, L., Candelon, F., & Lakhani, K. R. 2023. *Navigating the jagged technological frontier: Field experimental evidence of the effects of AI on knowledge worker productivity and quality*. Working Paper 24-013, Harvard Business School.

135 Li, Miaomiao, Yang Yu, and Jielin Yin. "Employee–AI collaboration empowers mentor networks to enhance employee creativity: a knowledge-management perspective." *Frontiers in Psychology* 17 (2026): 1750869.

produces a piece of work with significant AI assistance, their visible contribution becomes genuinely ambiguous: to their organization, to their manager, and sometimes to themselves. This is quieter and more personal than the familiar "*will AI take my job*" concern. It is about what their name on a piece of work means, and whether the professional reputation they are building reflects something real about them. Writing in the *Harvard Business Review*, Gratton has observed that many of the developmental experiences that shaped senior professionals' careers are at risk of being engineered away by tools that short-circuit the learning process.[136] That anxiety, in its most personal form, sits in your mentee's head when they hand in something an AI helped them write.

Most mentees will not raise this unprompted. The question that tends to open the conversation is not "*are you worried about AI?*", that is too abstract. Something closer to the point is: "*When you hand in a piece of work that AI helped you draft, how do you feel about putting your name on it?*" That question lands differently. It gives the mentee permission to speak honestly rather than to be professionally appropriate.

It is also worth considering what AI cannot do. It cannot notice that your mentee seems flat today and ask what is really going on. It cannot share a story from its own career that reframes a problem the mentee thought was unique to them. It cannot hold a mentee to account for commitments made three weeks ago or push back on a decision that looks strategically sound on paper but feels wrong given what you know about that person in that organization. The human, relational, contextually-informed dimensions of mentoring are not incidental features of the

---

[136] Gratton, Lynda. 2025. "AI Is Changing How We Learn at Work." *Harvard Business Review*, December 22

relationship; they are its primary value. As AI becomes better at producing competent, generic guidance, the distinctive personal nature of a good mentoring relationship becomes more rather than less significant.

One practical note: some mentees will arrive at sessions having already consulted an AI tool about the issue they want to discuss. Treat it as you would any other preparation. Ask what the AI suggested, what rang true, and what felt off, and, most usefully, what the AI couldn't possibly have known about the situation that changes the picture. That third question is the one that does the real work. It reminds the mentee that they hold contextual knowledge that no tool can access, and it shifts the conversation from validating a generated answer to developing an informed judgment.

In which we pretend that technology is not the point

There is an uncomfortable truth that lies beneath any discussion of virtual mentoring: some experienced mentors are less comfortable with the technology than their mentees, and this imbalance, if unacknowledged, can quietly undermine the relationship. A mentor who is visibly struggling with screen sharing, whose audio cuts out repeatedly because they have not checked their microphone, or who spends the first ten minutes of a session apologizing for technical difficulties, is not projecting the calm, capable presence that effective mentoring requires. This is not about being a technology expert. It is about being sufficiently competent that the technology becomes invisible, leaving the conversation itself at the center of the session.

The baseline is modest but non-negotiable. A stable internet connection, a working microphone, adequate lighting so your mentee can read your face, and a background that does not distract, these are the equivalents of turning up to an in-person meeting on time and in appropriate dress. They signal that you have prepared and that you take the session seriously. Beyond the basics, familiarity with whichever platform your organization uses, Zoom, Teams, or Google Meet, matters enough to warrant occasional deliberate practice. If you wouldn't walk into a room without knowing how to open the door, don't start a virtual mentoring session without knowing how to turn on your camera.

Session structure deserves particular attention in a virtual context. Research by Nurmi & Pakarinen found that virtual meetings tend to produce a specific type of fatigue that many people do not anticipate: not exhaustion from overload, but drowsiness from under-stimulation.[137] In other words, the problem with long virtual sessions is not that they demand too much, but that they offer too little: the physical passivity, the restricted field of view, and the absence of the ambient social cues that keep us alert in person all conspire to reduce engagement over time. For mentors, this has practical implications: virtual sessions benefit from more deliberate structure and active prompts than their in-person counterparts. Build in natural pauses, check in on energy levels mid-session, and be willing to end when the conversation has reached a natural conclusion rather than filling the allocated time for its own sake.

The question of when to insist on video versus when to accept audio-only is worth thinking through in advance. Video adds significant value when you need to read emotional state, deliver difficult feedback, or work through something sensitive. Audio

---

[137] Nurmi, N., & Pakarinen, S. 2023. "Virtual meeting fatigue: Exploring the impact of virtual meetings on cognitive performance and active versus passive fatigue." *Journal of Occupational Health Psychology* 28, no. 6: 343–362.

is often perfectly adequate for follow-up conversations or sessions where the mentee primarily needs to think out loud. Being flexible about format signals respect for your mentee's circumstances; not everyone has a private, well-lit space available at every meeting time.

Finally, consider asynchronous communication between sessions. Virtual mentoring opens options that don't exist in person: a voice note sent after a difficult week, a brief check-in message when something significant happens, a shared document for reflections between meetings. Used lightly and by mutual agreement, these tools maintain continuity without intruding. Establish early what level of between-session contact works for both parties and revisit it if circumstances change.

Exercise: The virtual mentoring health check

Most experienced mentors have a reasonably clear sense of how their face-to-face sessions are going. The virtual equivalent is harder to read. Without the physical cues: the body language, the energy in the room, the sense of whether your mentee left looking energized or fatigued than when they arrived: it is easy to finish a video call thinking it went well when it merely went smoothly. This exercise is designed to help you look more closely.

Work through the statements below and rate yourself honestly on a scale of 1 to 5, where 1 means rarely or never, and 5 means consistently and deliberately.

	1 - 5
I structure virtual sessions differently from face-to-face ones, recognizing they have a different energy and rhythm	

I am more deliberate about building rapport at the start of a virtual session than I would be in person	
I actively compensate for the loss of physical cues by asking more direct check-in questions during the session	
I share relevant organizational context that my mentee may be missing because of working remotely or away from the center of things	
I have a clear, mutually agreed understanding with my mentee about between-session contact: what is welcome, what is not, and through which channel	
I make a deliberate effort to bridge the information and visibility gap when my mentee and I have different working arrangements: for example, one office-based, one remote	
I vary the session format, video, audio, and shorter check-ins, based on what each conversation requires, rather than defaulting to the same setup every time	
I am genuinely comfortable discussing AI tools and their impact on my mentee's work and career, rather than avoiding the topic	
I notice when a virtual session is losing energy or focus, and I do something about it rather than pushing through to the end	
I give the same quality of attention in virtual sessions that I would in person: phone away, notifications off, fully present	
Total	

What your score suggests

Add up your scores. If you scored over 45, congratulations, you have an opportunity to write a book documenting your experiences! Between 36 and 45, and your virtual mentoring practice is probably in good health, though any individual statement where you scored 3 or below is worth specific attention. Between 20 and 35, there are some meaningful gaps worth addressing. Below 20, and virtual mentoring may be working less well than you think.

One final note of caution about high scores: the most revealing question is not how you rate yourself, but how your mentee would rate you. If you are not sure, ask them!

Debrief

The fundamentals of good mentoring do not change with the medium. What changes is the effort required to make them work. Virtual mentoring that merely replicates a face-to-face session on a smaller rectangle will always feel like a lesser version. Virtual mentoring, designed for its context, structured differently, with explicit attention to rapport, energy, and what the camera cannot show you, can be every bit as good. Remember, research suggests that if you let the session drift, your mentee will be drowsy rather than exhausted, which is perhaps the most counterintuitive finding in the entire field of organizational psychology. As for AI, it is in the room whether you invite it or not. Your mentee is using it. The question is not whether to acknowledge this, but how to make it productive. The mentor who can help a mentee think critically about what AI produces, manage anxiety about what it might displace, and hold on to the developmental experiences that no algorithm can yet replace is doing something that matters. Possibly more than ever.

Your next step: Do the virtual mentoring health check: honestly, not optimistically. Then, in your next session with your mentee, ask them directly: How well is our virtual mentoring working for you? Not "is everything okay?" Ask specifically. You may be surprised by the answer. You may also find it is the most useful conversation you have had in a while.

18. Conclusion: Now go and do it

You have read the manual... Now put it down

TL;DR:

You have reached the end of the book. You now know more about mentoring than most people who are doing it. The question is no longer whether you understand what good mentoring looks like: it is whether you are going to do something about it. Go and find your mentee. The rest will follow.

What you now know (and what to do with it)

Here is the truth about everything you have just read: knowing it is not the same as doing it.

You could have absorbed every chapter, highlighted every framework, and completed every self-assessment in this book, and still walk into your first mentoring session and promptly forget half of it under the mild pressure of an actual human being sitting across from you with an actual problem. This is not a failure of memory or commitment. It is simply what happens when theory meets practice, and it happens to everyone.

The good news is that this book was never about giving you a system to memorize. It was about helping you develop judgment, the kind of situational awareness that lets you read what a mentee needs in each moment rather than defaulting to whatever worked last time, or whatever you read in chapter four. Frameworks are useful. Judgment is better. And judgment, unlike frameworks, cannot be acquired from a book. It accumulates through practice, reflection, and the occasional humbling session where you realize you gave entirely the wrong advice with entirely too much confidence.

The invitation at the end of this book is not to feel ready. It starts before you feel ready: because the readiness, it turns out, only comes after you begin.

The skilled improviser, revisited

The central argument of this book is that effective mentors are skilled improvisers: prepared but not rigid, experienced but not formulaic, confident but genuinely curious about each new person they encounter. Jazz musicians do not play the same solo twice. Good mentors do not run the same session twice, either, not because they are being deliberately creative, but because their mentees are different people with different needs at different moments, and paying attention to that is the job.

What makes an improviser skilled rather than merely unpredictable is exactly what this book has tried to build: a repertoire of techniques, a capacity for active listening, an ability to ask the question that matters rather than the one that comes first to mind, and the self-awareness to know when your instincts are serving your mentee and when they are serving your own comfort.

You now have the repertoire. The rest is practice.

A final word

Mentoring is one of the most worthwhile ways a leader can spend their time. It is also, occasionally, frustrating, ambiguous, and stubbornly resistant to the feeling that you are doing it right. Some sessions will end, and you will have no idea whether anything useful happened. Some mentees will take your most carefully crafted insight and completely ignore it, then, six months later, tell someone else it was the best advice they ever received, with no mention of where they heard it. This is fine. It is, in fact, that's the job.

The measure of good mentoring is not whether your mentee follows your advice. It is whether they leave each conversation slightly better able to think through their own challenges than when they arrived. If that is happening, even imperfectly, even intermittently, you are doing it.

Nobody becomes a great mentor by reading about mentoring. They become one by showing up, paying attention, occasionally getting it wrong, and caring enough to keep going. You clearly care enough. You read an entire book about it!

Now put it down and go find someone to help.

Appendices:

Practical exercises for mentors

Appendices A and B are standalone worksheets from specific chapters. Appendix A reproduces the Career Vision template from Chapter 4; Appendix B reproduces the Mentoring Action Plan from Chapter 13. Both are included here so they can be printed, photocopied, or shared with mentees without the surrounding chapter text interfering. They require no further introduction. You will find all the necessary context in the chapters themselves.

Appendix C is of a different nature. The Improviser's Toolkit is not associated with any single chapter. The theme of the skilled improviser runs throughout the entire book, and the exercises in Appendix C are designed to develop the foundational abilities, presence, adaptability, and comfort with ambiguity that the book describes but cannot, on its own, cultivate. Reading about improvisation is somewhat like reading about swimming. At some point, you need to get into the water. If you want to do that, Appendix C is the best place to start — at the end of the book!

Appendix A: Career Vision template

<table>
<tr>
<td rowspan="2">A career vision statement describes what the world might look like and feel like as a result of your professional work. A clear, compelling vision can have a magnetic effect – prioritizing choices and pulling you towards it as you focus on your work.

Your vision statement will answer: "WHAT do I want to be part of in 5 years' time?"

My Vision Statement:

Why do you want to achieve this?</td>
<td rowspan="2">Strengths & Weaknesses.
Strengths are those factors that accelerate your trajectory towards your vision.
Weaknesses are those factors that may hold you back from attaining your vision. When thinking about your weaknesses, it's important to view yourself from other people's perspectives because other people tend to notice things about you that you are blind to. Although this can be an uncomfortable task, it's vital that you see yourself as realistically as possible. To this end, it's important to ask people who know you best what areas you need to improve.</td>
<th>Strengths</th>
<th>Weaknesses</th>
</tr>
<tr>
<td>• What are you better at than other people?
• What do other people view as your strengths?
• How much experience do you have in your profession?
• What skills, abilities, knowledge, or connections do you have that others don't?
• What values do you live by that most people find too demanding?
• Which professional achievements are you proudest of?</td>
<td>• What do other people say your weaknesses are?
• Which activities do you avoid doing, and why do you dislike doing them?
• Do you struggle with anxiety, imposter syndrome, or procrastination?
• Are there gaps in your education, skills, or training?
• Are you afraid to take risks?</td>
</tr>
</table>

Appendix B: Mentoring Action Plan worksheet

Personal vision: (~5 years)		
Goals & objectives		
1.		
2.		
3.		
4.		
Goal 1:	Development Activity 1:	
	Development Activity 2:	
	Development Activity 3:	
Goal 2:	Development Activity 1:	
	Development Activity 2:	
	Development Activity 3:	
Goal 3:	Development Activity 1:	
	Development Activity 2:	
	Development Activity 3:	

Appendix C: The Improviser's Toolkit

The skilled improviser metaphor runs through every chapter of this book. This appendix turns the metaphor into practice. The exercises below are drawn from applied improvisation, a discipline that adapts theatrical improv techniques for non-performance contexts, including business, education, and healthcare.[138] They are not about being funny or performing. They are about developing the mental agility, presence, and responsiveness that distinguish a good mentor from a formulaic one.

Research supports this connection directly. A National Science Foundation–funded study developed an improvisation-based workshop specifically to build empathy and effective communication in mentor–mentee relationships, finding that improv exercises improved the quality of mentoring interactions and increased awareness of interpersonal dynamics.[139] Controlled studies have demonstrated that improv training yields measurable gains in creativity, divergent thinking, tolerance for uncertainty, and self-efficacy, precisely the capacities that effective mentoring demands.

You do not need any performance experience to use these exercises. You need only a willingness to try something that may

---

[138]Cunha, M.P., Vera, D., Abrantes, A.C.M. & Miner, A.S. (Eds.). 2024. *The Routledge Companion to Improvisation in Organizations*. London: Routledge.

[139]O'Connell, C., McCauley, J., & Herbert, L. 2021. "Improvisation-Based Workshop to Build Empathy in Mentor-Mentee Relationships and Support Academic Equity. *Journal of Student Affairs Research and Practice* 59: 87-100. https://doi.org/10.1080/19496591.2020.1842747

feel slightly uncomfortable at first, and the recognition that discomfort and learning often go hand in hand.

Divergent and convergent thinking

Before the exercises, one framework. The psychologist J.P. Guilford identified two complementary modes of thinking that underpin creative problem-solving: **divergent thinking**, generating multiple possibilities without premature judgment, and **convergent thinking**, evaluating and selecting the best option from those possibilities.[140] Effective mentoring conversations move between both modes. The trouble is that most of us default to convergent thinking too early: we hear a problem and immediately narrow in on a solution before the problem has been properly explored.

Improv techniques are, at their core, tools for divergent thinking.[141] They keep the conversation open, generative, and exploratory long enough for the real issue and the real options to emerge. The GROW model from Chapter 9 provides the convergent structure. Combine the two, and you have a complete mentoring conversation: explore widely, then focus sharply.

Exercise 1: 'Yes, and...' for mentors

Purpose: To build on your mentee's contributions rather than redirecting them prematurely.

Time: Ongoing (*this is a practice, not a one-off exercise*)

---

[140] Guilford, J.P. 1967. *The Nature of Human Intelligence*. New York: McGraw-Hill.

[141] Kulhan, B. with Crisafulli, C. 2017. *Getting to "Yes And": The Art of Business Improv*. Stanford, CA: Stanford University Press.

How it works: In your next mentoring session, commit to responding to your mentee's first three statements with '*Yes, and...*' rather than '*Yes, but...*' or '*Have you considered...?*' This does not mean agreeing with everything. It means receiving what they offer, building on it, and then introducing your own perspective. If your mentee says, '*I think I should apply for the role even though I don't meet all the criteria,*' a '*Yes, but*' response might be: '*Yes, but you're missing two years of experience.*' A '*Yes, and*' response might be: '*Yes, and what would you say to the panel about the experience you do have?*' The first closes the conversation down. The second opens it up.

What to notice: Pay attention to how often your instinct is to correct, qualify, or redirect. Most experienced professionals find they default to '*Yes, but*' far more often than they realize. Also, notice what happens to your mentee's energy when you build on their idea rather than qualifying it: they typically become more engaged, more willing to think out loud, and more likely to self-correct without being told to.

Exercise 2: Active listening reset

Purpose: To listen to what your mentee is saying rather than preparing your response while they speak.

Time: First five minutes of a mentoring session.

How it works: For the opening five minutes of your next session, do nothing but listen and reflect. When your mentee finishes a thought, summarize what you heard in your own words before asking a question or offering a response. '*So, what I'm hearing is...*' or '*It sounds like the core issue is...*' Do not add your interpretation, your advice, or your similar experience. Just mirror. If you have captured it accurately, your mentee will say so and usually elaborate further, often reaching the real issue without any prompting from you. If you have not captured it accurately, they will correct you, which is equally valuable: you now know what they meant rather than what you assumed.

What to notice: This exercise is harder than it sounds. You will feel the pull to jump in, to problem-solve, to share your own experience. That pull is your convergent thinking trying to take over before the divergent phase is complete. Resist it for five minutes and see what emerges.

Exercise 3: Making your mentee look good

Purpose: To build your mentee's confidence by helping them experience their own competence.

Time: Throughout any mentoring session.

How it works: In improvisation, the cardinal rule is to make your scene partner look good. The equivalent in mentoring is to ask questions you sense your mentee can answer well, then let them answer. When they articulate a half-formed idea, reflect it back to them in slightly more structured language: '*So what you're describing is essentially a stakeholder mapping exercise, that's a smart instinct.*' You are not inventing competence that is not there. You are naming competence that is there, but that your mentee has not yet recognized. When your mentee has a genuine insight during a conversation, say so explicitly: '*That's a sharp observation, can you take that further?*' Then get out of the way.

What to notice: This is different from praise. Praise is '*Well done.*' Making your mentee look good means creating the conditions for them to demonstrate their capabilities and ensuring they notice they did. The first builds dependence on the mentor's approval. The second builds self-efficacy.

Exercise 4: Staying present

Purpose: To respond to what is happening in the room rather than following your prepared agenda.

Time: A single mentoring session.

How it works: Before your next session, prepare as you normally would: review your notes, think about where the conversation might go. Then, when the session begins, set your notes aside. Physically. If your mentee raises something that was not on the agenda, follow it. If they seem distracted or lower in energy than usual, name it: '*You seem like something else is on your mind today, do you want to talk about that instead?*' Improvisers call this 'reading the room, ' and it is the single most transferable skill from improvisation to mentoring. It requires you to pay attention to tone, body language, energy, and the gap between what your mentee is saying and what they seem to mean.

What to notice: Notice your own anxiety when the conversation departs from your plan. That anxiety is natural: it is your brain telling you that structure is being lost. But some of the most productive mentoring conversations happen precisely when the plan is abandoned in favor of what the mentee needs right now. Your preparation is not wasted; it is what gives you the confidence to improvise when the moment calls for it.

Exercise 5: Embracing the offer

Purpose: To treat unexpected or uncomfortable moments as opportunities rather than problems.

Time: Whenever something surprising happens in a session.

How it works: In improv, everything that happens on stage is called an 'offer', including mistakes, misunderstandings, and unexpected contributions. The improviser's job is to accept and use whatever is offered rather than blocking it. In mentoring, this translates directly. When your mentee says something you were not expecting, a confession of doubt, a challenge to your advice, or a sudden change of direction, treat it as an offer. Lean into it rather than steering back to safer ground. '*That's interesting, tell me more about that*' is almost always more productive than '*Let's come back to what we were discussing.*' The unexpected moment is often where the real learning happens.

What to notice: Pay attention to the moments when you feel the urge to redirect the conversation back to familiar territory. That urge is a signal that something important may be emerging: something that your mentee has not yet felt safe enough, or clear enough, to raise directly. The offer is usually hiding just beneath the surface.

Putting it together

These five exercises are not separate techniques to be deployed one at a time. They are facets of a single capacity: the ability to be fully present with another person and to respond to what they need rather than what you planned to provide. That capacity is what this book calls the skilled improviser.

If you want to develop it deliberately, start with one exercise per session for the next five sessions. After each session, spend two minutes reflecting: What did I notice? What was harder than expected? What happened differently because I tried this? You will not master any of these in a single attempt. That is the point. Like the jazz musician practicing scales, the value is in the repetition, not the perfection.

One final observation. You may have noticed that every exercise in this appendix asks you to do *less* rather than more: less advising, less redirecting, less planning, and less controlling the conversation. That is not a coincidence. The skilled improviser's greatest strength is not what they add to the conversation. It is what they allow to emerge.

About the Author

Robert Rosenfeld has been teaching managers how to lead since 1981, which means he has also spent four decades watching them ignore the advice and figure it out anyway. This book is for those managers and for those still working on it.

Over that time, he has worked with managers and leaders across more than 30 countries and 80 organizations worldwide, bringing both academic rigor and hard-won cross-cultural experience to every chapter. His work spans executive development, management education, and organizational consulting, with clients ranging from early-career managers to boards of major international organizations.

He has learned, sometimes the hard way, that the best mentors are not the ones with the most experience. They are the ones still willing to be surprised by the conversation before them.

Continue the conversation at www.corex.net

www.ingramcontent.com/pod-product-compliance
Lightning Source LLC
LaVergne TN
LVHW020707110826
845149LV00012B/2147